THE DEVIL'S ALPHABET

THE DEVIL'S ALPHABET

KURT E. KOCH

KREGEL PUBLICATIONS
Grand Rapids, Michigan 49501

The Devil's Alphabet, by Kurt E. Koch, translated from the German by Evangelizations Publishers, West Germany, 1969. Published in the United States of America by Kregel Publications, a division of Kregel, Inc. P. O. Box 2607, Grand Rapids, MI 49501. All rights reserved. First Kregel Publications edition: 1971.

Library of Congress Catalog Card No. LC-76-160692

ISBN   0-8254-3004-6 (pbk.)

6 7 8 9 Printing/Year 93 92

Printed in the United States of America

Contents

Preface

The devil is a many-sided and versatile demagogue. To the psychologist he says, "I will give you new knowledge and understanding." To the occultist he will say, "I will give you the keys to the last secrets of creation." He confronts the religionist and the moralist with a mask of integrity and promises them the very help of heaven. And finally to the rationalist and the liberalist he says, "I am not there. I do not even exist."

The devil is a skillful strategist. He is the master of every tactic of the battle field. He befogs the front. He hides behind a camouflage of empty religious talk. He operates through the use of the latest scientific method. He successfully fires and launches his arguments on the social and humane plane. And his sole aim is to deceive, to entice, and to ensnare his victims.

Who then, we ask, is sufficient for these things? Who can withstand such a strategist and tactician? Only the One who has ventured all in His battle against the prince of darkness. It was He who repulsed the devil in the wilderness. It was He who destroyed the veil of darkness, and who became the Saviour of Calvary, having defeated all the powers of Satan. We hear the triumphant cry of Paul as he writes in Col. 2:15,

> Christ has disarmed the principalities and powers,
> He has made an open example of them,
> He has triumphed over them in His cross.

It is to Christ then that we look. To Him all power has been given. In everything He must have the pre-eminence (Col. 1:18).

In the course of reading this book you will find that reference has often been made to actual case histories in order to substantiate and illustrate the phenomenon and effects of superstition and occultism. I would like to point out then at the very outset that these examples are drawn from my own counselling experience and, unless it is specifically mentioned to the contrary, I have myself actually talked with one or more of the persons concerned in each example.

The Author

Preface to the Fourth Edition

This is now the fourth edition of this book, and it has been expanded to include the five new sections on Colour Therapy, Firewalking, Telepathy, Tongues Movements, and Umbanda and Macumba.

In the world today an increasing flood of occult movements tries to overrule the Church of Christ. We live in the last phase of the end of the age. We have therefore to raise our heads and to look for the Coming Lord to whom all power in heaven, upon earth and under the earth is given. The battle is won. The victory is His. Empowered by this fact we can dare to face all the onslaughts of the defeated foe.

Kurt Koch

I. The Standpoint of our Assessment of Superstitious and Occult Customs

Superstition is the greatest contaminater of the soul of all time, stemming as it does from fear and the desire for power. "By superstition we mean the dependence of certain inexplicable forces and phenomena, not governed by the usual natural laws, on the psychical, or in other words, the belief that certain events are causally connected with things which are apparently completely unrelated to them." This is how Dr. Schrank defines the real essence of superstition (Psychologie des Aberglaubens im Riedel-Archiv). Superstition and faith stand in sharp contrast to one another even though their descriptions conform somewhat to the ideological and religious ideas of the person assessing them. For example, the Buddhist or the Moslem would relegate the Christian faith to the level of superstition and heresy. We must therefore make it clear from the very start from what standpoint we are going to discuss this subject.

Whatever the Christian Church understands by superstition is made known to it through Christ. For us Jesus Christ is the divider of spirits. He is the immovable rock on which the ever changing waves of ideological opinion break. Everything motivated by Christ is faith, everything which Christ opposes is superstition. That is the widest standard by which we can assess superstitious ideas. Our guide lines are not drawn from the principles of the physical sciences alone, but from the Word of God.

This assertion already introduces us to an important
line of demarcation. Anyone reading scientific literature
published against superstition will at once recognise that
the viewpoint taken is very different from that of Christianity. Science only recognises natural laws and purely
human concepts. It is glued to the material world. And this
is justifiable, for it only claims to deal with the intelligible
and the rational. The supernatural, the transcendental, the
demonic and the divine are closed to its investigations.
Science can only hope to understand those things which can
be brought within its own narrow rationalistic limits.
Because of this the demonic has often been dragged down
to the level of the reason and hence explained away. And
so we cannot rely upon science for a true explanation of
superstition. It also follows that the scientist's means of
defence is entirely insufficient. This is clearly illustrated
in Johann Kruse's book *Hexen unter uns?* From the point
of view of the material it contains, this book is one of the
most informative works on superstition today. However,
the author generally takes the line that there are no genuine
phenomena connected with superstition. He fails to recognise its true background for he would otherwise not have
called charming and spell-casting a harmless practice.

Science on the other hand is not so much interested in
explaining superstition away as in looking for the answer
in depth psychology. Dr. Schrank for example, considers
an apparition to be the projection of a person's subconscious. He also suggests that an ordinary group of people
may have an audible and visual experience of an apparition
when suffering from what one might call a collective
hallucination. This may indeed be the explanation in a
number of cases. Jänsch's teaching on eidetic images and
Jung's theory of archetypes indicate the possibility of such
an interpretation. However, on the other hand, Christian

teaching recognises facts and dimensions beyond the range of the purely scientific mind.

Superstition is not only a sign of stupidity, credulity and a lack of knowledge and enlightenment, but it is also a sign of a bias towards God-opposed forces. The human race is torn between two great powers and is too weak to maintain its neutrality. It is good to remember the saying: to close the door to faith is to open the door to superstition. To put it another way, if we reject God, Satan himself will plague us. Paul the apostle put it even more clearly when he said in Eph. 6:12, "We are not contending against flesh and blood, but against the principalities, against the powers, against the world rulers of this present darkness, against the spiritual hosts of wickedness in the heavenly places." As Christians we know of the reality of these powers. However, in saying this we must not go to the other extreme and label everything we cannot understand as demonic. We may still as Christians make use of the findings of science, for this lies within God's original command to man to subdue the earth (Gen. 1:28). But science has no right to have the last word and it is sheer presumption on the part of the scientist who makes this claim.

Although there are two powers opposed to one another in this world, it does not mean that people are being dragged to and fro quite helplessly between them. No, Archimedes' wish to have a fixed point of reference independent of the earth, and that implies beyond the reach of science, has been realised. The cross of Christ stands in the world witnessing to the fact that He has made an end to all the powers of darkness. The psalmist's triumphant song has reached its fulfillment; "Hark, glad songs of victory in the tents of the righteous: the right hand of the Lord does valiantly, the right hand of the Lord is exalted, the right hand of the Lord does valiantly" (Ps. 118:15f). Death and hell have been robbed of their power. So with this victory behind him, a person can confidently speak out clearly concerning demonic powers, knowing that Christ has taken the last vestiges of their strength away. We know the terror of these powers of Satan, but we also know that through Christ no harm can befall us. It is to us that the Word of the Lord has been given as a shield, "Behold, I have given you authority over all the power of the enemy; and nothing shall hurt you." So with our eyes fixed firmly on Jesus we can approach the devil's alphabet. The fear of the Lord overcomes the fear of Satan.

II. The Devil's Alphabet

Amulets. The custom of wearing amulets (Arabic: *hamalet* = appendage) has gone on for thousands of years all over the world. The native wears a tiger's claw to gain the animal's strength. The European nails a horse shoe over his door for luck. There are people who wear lucky charms on their watch chains. In Switzerland some of the men wear small gold ear-rings as a protection against eye infection. The driver carries a mascot or talisman (Arabic: *tilsam* = magic picture) with him in the car, while the pilot takes a small animal such as a dog or canary on board with him for luck. Many soldiers used to carry letters of protection about with them in the hope that this would make them bullet-proof. Yet no matter what the custom is, each and every one of them is just a pitiable effort to compensate for a lack of faith in God.

Anthroposophy. Anthroposophy, founded by Rudolf Steiner, has as its aim the exploration of human nature. It involves exercises in concentration designed to lead to the mastery of thought and will and to arouse the latent occult forces in man. Through a process of clairvoyance one is meant to attain to a vision of the transcendental world and one's former existences. The biblical way of salvation through faith in the Redeemer is replaced by the way of mystical visions. One of the principle doctrines of anthroposophy is the belief in reincarnation. Man is supposed to be reborn into the world once every 800 years. I would like to give two examples in connection with this idea.

1. A Swedish professor made the following experiment using hypnosis. He questioned his subject on matters relating to her childhood and early life and then went one step

further and asked her about events which had taken place
before she had been born. Under hypnosis the woman was
able to make exact statements which were later confirmed
to be true by reference to some official records. People who
believe in reincarnation would say that this is evidence in
support of their belief.

2. Driving from Munich to Karlsruhe on the autobahn I
was stopped by a man who asked me for a lift. When he
had got into the car we began to talk to each other and I
asked him about his occupation. He told me that he was
an anthroposophical priest. I asked him about the central
point of his beliefs and he said that it was reincarnation.
He went on to say that according to their religion man
returns to this life every 800 years. It is sometimes possible,
so he said, to tell what a person was 800 years ago through
various inclinations, preferences and tendencies of the present. I said I would be interested to know what I had been
800 years ago, so the priest asked me about what I was
prejudiced against. In order to mislead him I said that
clergymen made me mad. His reply was immediate. "800
years ago you were a professor of theology." I still today
fail to see the logic of his conclusion.

I am well aware of the fact that one cannot dispose of
anthroposophy in just a few sentences. If anyone wishes to
go into the matter more thoroughly I can recommend
Hutten's book, *Seher, Gruebler und Enthusiasten (Seers,
Thinkers and Enthusiasts).* For the moment we have only
time for a rough outline. It has been demonstrated that
Steiner's teaching is a strange mixture of Indian, gnostic,
occult, theosophical, idealistic and Christian thought, which
though quite fascinating, is still a dangerous and erronious
doctrine.

After the publication of the first edition of this book I
encountered a former friend of Rudolf Steiner who told

me, "I have some circular letters of Steiner in which he gives advice and rules on how to practise table-lifting. On being confronted by this spiritistic practice I left the movement." An experience of this nature should open the blind eyes of those people who are members of Anthroposophy.

Astrology. In this colourful folkdance of superstition we now come to astrology. In his book *Psychologie des Aberglaubens*, Dr. Schrank writes, "When the leading astrologer Werle describes astrology as mantic or the art of fortune-telling, he consciously leaves the firm ground of science for the swamp of superstition. We can see how dangerous it is by the way in which serious psychic disturbances, a fear of life, despair and derangement are produced by it in sensitive people. Astrology paralyzes initiative and powers of judgement. It stupifies and encourages shallowness. It moulds the personality into receiving an underground movement that thrives on platitudes." If a doctor and scientist has recognised these effects, then I need not substantiate them again here. Nevertheless I would like to recount two of the most recent examples I have come across in my work.

3. After giving two lectures in Strasbourg I was approached by a French minister who told me the following story. A psychology student at the Sorbonne University in Paris had wanted to write a thesis for his doctor's degree on the subject of the psychology of superstition. To help him in this task he put an advertisement in a newspaper stating that he was an astrologer. He promised to send a detailed horoscope to anyone who requested one for a prepaid fee of about 30 shillings. The young man received a number of replies and with the proceeds he was able to finance his studies at the university. He cast only one horoscope for all his clients basing it upon the principle

that every statement in it must be as ambiguous as possible.
On top of this he included the suggestion of positive character traits, this being what everyone wants to believe.
And so each applicant received exactly the same horoscope.
Afterwards the student was showered with letters of ap-
preciation. He then wrote his doctor's thesis. His experiment had been a complete success.

4. A young man consulted an astrologer. The astrologer
cast a detailed horoscope for him which included the statement that he would marry while he was still quite young.
However, it also stated that his first wife would not be the
one destined for him, and that a second wife would be the
one to bring him real happiness. As it happened the young
man soon married. On his wedding day he turned to his
elder brother and said, "The woman I'm marrying today
is not the right one. My second wife will be the one to
make me happy but I've got to marry this woman first in
order to find her." Just imagine under what misapprehen-
sions this young man was getting married. It turned out
that this first woman made him a very good wife and she
soon won the affection of her parents-in-law. In the first
three years of their marriage she bore him three children
but after the birth of the third child the husband left her.
Later he obtained a divorce on the grounds of his own com-
plicity. He then found the second woman who, according
to the horoscope, was destined to make him happy. But
this was only true for a few months. His new wife became
a fanatical member of the Jehovah's Witnesses. He was
utterly opposed to the fanatical behaviour of his wife, and
so he left her too and again obtained a divorce. He had
been the victim of an astrological assertion which had
influenced him suggestively.

Let us now listen to what the Astronomical Society officially said about astrology in 1949:

"The Astronomical Society takes the opportunity of this present conference in Bonn to expressly warn people against the continuing spread of the evils of astrology. The belief that the position of the stars at the moment of a person's birth influences their life in any way, and that man can consult the stars in matters relating to his public or private life, has its origin in the ancient astronomical idea that this world, together with the human race, is situated at the very centre of the cosmos. This concept, however, disappeared long ago. Whatever hides behind the title of astrology or cosmo-biology today, is nothing more than a mixture of superstition, duplicity and business.

It is true, there are astrological circles which have disassociated themselves from the standardized and printed character analyses and predictions which are made to cover almost all aspects of human life. However, these people instead erect their own 'scientific' astrologies which one is supposed to take seriously. It still cannot be demonstrated that these new astrologies are related in any way to science and to scientific methods. A few chance fulfilments of some astrological predictions cannot alter the matter. Astrology is merely comprised of an assumed random set of rules. Such a system cannot claim to give scientifically based interpretations and forecasts in either public or private matters.

Observatories, and the astronomers who work in them, are repeatedly being asked, both by private individuals and by official agencies, to give their opinions on astrology. These opinions cannot differ from those being publically expressed here by the Astronomical Society."

A t h e i s m . Atheism introduces us to yet another bulwark of superstition. Most atheists are inconsistent. It is true that they have thrown a belief in God overboard. However, they instead often become slaves of superstition, and the life of Voltaire, one of the world's greatest cynics, is an indication of this. Generally speaking, the lives and the families of militant atheists do not present one with a happy picture.

5. A young man came to me for counselling. He told me that his family had over the years been plagued by many serious accidents and psychic abnormalities. I asked him if there was any history of mental illness or occult subjection in the family, but he replied in the negative. However, the following facts came to light. His grandfather had been a wholesaler near Hamburg. He had been an appalling blasphemer and cynic. He had tried at every opportunity to drag Christianity through the mud through writing articles against it or through argument. The mental heritage left by the grandfather had had some terrible effects on the descendents.

6. An atheist wrote a book pouring contempt on the Christian religion. None of his descendants are normal. His children were either born with crippled legs or were crippled later in life through illness. Some of the children are also mentally retarded, and some of the grandchildren have suffered in the same way. Besides this, all his descendants are moody, they suffer from depressions and are all confessed atheists — "Be not deceived; God is not mocked" (Gal. 6:7).

This story was told to me by one of the granddaughters living in Switzerland. Unbelief and superstition invariably mean that the person concerned hands himself over to powers opposed to God, and these powers then use the person's life as a stage for their own revelations.

Black and White Magic. The art of black and white magic has the devil's very own stamp on it and goes back over thousands of years. Magic in its origin and effects lies on a different level from that understood by scientific laws. It belongs to the domain of the mediumistic world order. However, because of its often harmless disguise its demonic nature is on many occasions not recognised. The words are apt, "Satan disguises himself as an angel of light" (2 Cor. 11:14). On innumerable occasions people have raised the objection, "Oh yes, black magic is the work of the devil, but white magic relies on good forces." This confusion is so wide-spread that a book written for doctors on the mission field, after admitting that the Africans can be helped through black magic and juju, advised the missionaries to counteract this by using white magic. This is a terrible misjudgement of white magic. What is happening to our missionary work today if things like this are being published? Opinions such as this, together with white magic itself, are proved wrong by the effects. Since I have already gone into the question of magic quite fully in my book *Between Christ and Satan,* a detailed account is not necessary here. However, we will just mention the most frequent areas of magic. These are: healing and causing diseases; love and hate magic; persecution and defence magic; making and breaking spells; death magic. Some examples will help introduce us to this terrible world of demonic activity.

7. A woman who was seriously ill was given no hope of recovery by two specialists. The family was informed that she would soon die. On hearing this, her husband called on the dangerous magic charmer Hugentobler from Peterzell for help. The woman's condition immediately improved and she got better. However, she later made three attempts to commit suicide. Because of this she went to a Christian minister to be counselled. A prayer group was subsequently formed for her and by the grace of God she was completely freed from the temptations.

8. A man was treated by an ill-famed magical charmer from Maria Einsiedel, Switzerland. The patient was interested in the charmer's powers of healing and asked him how he was able to heal people. The charmer replied, "It's ruining me, but I must do it as long as I live."

9. A 62-year-old man visited the two charmers Hugentobler and Schneider. Since then he has suffered from a weakness of memory, and an inability to concentrate and to work. He was helped organically, but instead, he developed both psychical and nervous disturbances.

10. As a boy a man was treated by a magician. As a result of this he was organically healed but he afterwards began to be greatly troubled by his sex life and he is now lacking completely in self-control.

11. A married man courted a single girl. She refused to have anything to do with him saying that because he was married nothing could come of it. He threatened her saying, "Even though you don't want to, I can still get what I am after. I can get just what I want." From then on the woman frequently had experiences at night as if she was being sexually molested by the man although the doors and windows were locked. She was as if paralysed and could do nothing to defend herself. She realised at once that something was wrong. She came to be counselled and confessed what was troubling her.

12. A 19-year-old girl was one night frightened out of her sleep. Although the doors and windows were closed she found herself being molested by a young man. She at once knew that this was something unnatural. She was unable to cry for help and felt as if she was paralysed. Next day at the convalescent home in which she worked she met a young man. She recognised him at once to be the intruder of the previous night. The young man addressed

her and admitted quite openly, "I was with you last night. My grandmother taught me black magic and love magic. But I'm terribly burdened by it and want to be freed from it." He went on to admit that he could get anything he wanted through black magic.

13. A woman is plagued in a sexual way by a strange figure at night. It is a physical experience. If she prays in the name of Christ the force leaves her. Her father had similar experiences when he was young. At nights he was scratched by cats. In the morning he had scratches on his hands and throat.

These last three examples are not just cases of sexual halluzination. When schizophrenics pray in the name of Christ their oppressions do not disappear. On the other hand an appeal in the name of Christ is of immediate help in the case of magical molesting.

14. A woman had a new pram stolen. She thus went to the occult practitioner Hungerbühler. The pram returned within three days. However, the woman afterwards suffered from a compulsion neurosis. She would also have very bad depressions before Easter and Christmas each year.

15. A minister on the German island of Rügen in the Baltic Sea told me that a so-called 'thief blessing' exists there. Certain people in some way or other are able to give a 'thief blessing' to the fishing nets or baskets. If a thief tries at night to steal the fish he is put under a kind of ban and is unable to leave the baskets. Thus the owners are able to catch the thief in the morning.

16. A woman in Switzerland came to be counselled. She said that as a child she had been terribly plagued at night. The stables also on their farm had suffered extensive damage and a few days before Christmas and Easter each year the cattle, pigs and chickens had all died. Her father had

gone to the well-know charmer from Teufen, Schneider. Schneider put some defence magic into operation. Immediately after this a neighbour's wife who was suspected of practising black magic became insane. Thereafter no more animals died.

17. After her marriage a young woman developed serious psychical disturbances, although previously she had been quite alright. The disturbances were sometimes accompanied by a fever. She went to see a clairvoyant who turned out to be Hungerbühler. This man said to her, "You are bewitched. Your neighbour's plaguing you." The woman was unable to believe this and so went to a card-layer with the reputation of possessing supernatural powers. The card-layer had actually been jailed during the war for predicting three years before it happened that Hitler would be overthrown. Well, completely independently from the clairvoyant, the card-layer told the woman, "You've got a neighbour who is well versed in the art of black magic. He's working hand in hand with the devil and he's plaguing you." In the end the young woman had to be admitted into hospital because of her troubles. She was suffering from a permanent fever although the doctor could find no cause for it. The woman's husband now started a thorough investigation into the lives and activities of his neighbours. The only thing he could discover was that one of his neighbours practised the things contained in the 6th and 7th Book of Moses. Then one day another neighbour said to him, "Take care that nothing happens to your wife. The man in the house on your left has already ruined the wife of your predecessor. He's completely full of jealousy because the ground of your farm is good, while he has to slave all day on ground that is full of stones."

18. I know of one occult practitioner who is unable to help anyone who prays in his surgery. Whenever someone

does so he becomes furious and shouts things like, "I can't begin anything with you. Get out and go home." He told one woman in particular who prayed when with him, "Get out you old cow, and go home."

Blood Subscriptions. These are some of the most ghastly practices connected with superstition. A few examples.

19. A woman subscribed herself to the devil with her own blood. She belonged to a spiritistic circle with a membership of 15 people who consciously used to summon the devil to appear. Each time this happened a horrible figure manifested itself, and the members then indulged in an orgy. The woman acted as a medium for the group and, wherever she was, the leader could contact her by means of hypnosis. One day the woman came to an evangelistic meeting. She was challenged by the Word of God and made a general confession of the sins of her life. Immediately afterwards she was sorely troubled and tempted. She told me that at night she was regularly ordered to commit suicide. A continual state of extreme anxiety drove her to seek counselling help. One day she reported that the devil had imprinted a sign of ownership on her chest which she had shown to her sister. The mark was that of a horse shoe with the letter S in the middle of it. A group of people got together to pray for the poor woman. Some Christian psychiatrists were also consulted. These were all of the opinion that it was a case of possession and not mental illness.

20. Another woman on two occasions subscribed herself to the devil. When she became pregnant in the first year of her marriage she subscribed the unborn child to the devil as well. When the child was born it showed early signs of senility. Today although the child is only eight

years old it has already lost a lot of its hair and has developed wrinkles on its face like a woman of 50. The mother herself possesses mediumistic abilities. She has said in a trance that there are four devils in her. She has fits in which she is as strong as a bear. Once when a minister friend of mine visited her she grasped hold of him. However, when he cried, "I am protected by the blood of Christ", the woman was alarmed and let go again.

21. The daughter of a fortune-teller who laid cards subscribed herself to the devil several times as a young girl. At a mission she was confronted and awakened by the Word of God. She took the minister's advice and confessed her sins. But she was still unable to become a Christian. A dreadful conflict began within her between the powers of darkness and the Word of God. One day she read from Deut. 18 and she became so furious that she inked out the whole page in her Bible. The chapter itself speaks of charming, fortune-telling and sorcery etc. Afterwards she was upset about having disfigured her Bible and said that she had not really wanted to but a strange force had made her do it. A small group of people began to meet together to pray for her, but as yet the possessed young woman is still not free.

22. A man in one of the Alpine valleys had a flourishing business as a nature healer for years. He could cure people whom even the doctors had given up as hopeless. He could heal blind people, lame people and deaf people etc. One day in a thoughtful mood the man realised what a mess his life was in. Putting it in his own words he said, "I can help everybody else but for myself there will never be any help, not in all eternity." The man as a youth had subscribed himself to the devil. It was only since then that he had possessed his frightening powers of healing.

In my counselling experience I have only met two cases in which those who have taken part in blood subscriptions have ultimately been delivered from this terrible bondage by the grace of God.

Card-Laying. The use of card-laying as a means of fortune-telling is a widespread though doubtful practice. There are various forms of card-laying. There are the obviously fraudulent and money-making types, then the suggestive and telepathic fortune-telling types, and last but not least the mediumistic types of card-laying based on extrasensory and demonic faculties. Some examples.

23. A 49-year-old woman told me the following about her family. Both her mother-in-law and husband were Catholics. The mother-in-law was also a well-known card-layer. Her husband and children were strangely burdened. They suffered from depressions and fits of temper. The woman herself had been influenced by the uneasy attitude of her husband and mother-in-law. Whenever she wanted to go to church she started to vomit and got a headache. When her mother-in-law was dying she had to nurse her for a number of weeks. Her death was horrible. The other relatives must have lied to the priest when notifying him about the burial, because at the grave-side he described her as a 'saint'.

24. In the course of counselling, a young man said that he had married the daughter of a card-layer. The mother-in-law possessed some strange abilities. If ever a quarrel arose in the family and the young man did not support his mother-in-law he was afterwards plagued by her. His body would begin to itch all over and he would feel as if he had been bitten many times. No remedy could be found. It took him a long time to realise the cause of his troubles. His

mother-in-law could also foretell calamities. Once she said
to him, "A soldier will fall out of a window tonight and
be killed." He did not believe her at first, but a couple of
days later the newspaper carried a report of such an inci-
dent. She could also tell beforehand when an important
letter was about to arrive, and what the contents were.
The woman struck the young husband as being very strange
and he told this to a psychiatrist. In the end she was admitted to a clinic for nervous diseases on the recommendation
of the medical board. Nevertheless after this the young
man again began to suffer from the itching and the bites,
and still nothing could be found to alleviate his discomfort.

25. A young girl went to a woman who laid cards. She
was told by the woman that she would have an illegitimate
child, and that the child's father would later abandon her.
It so happened that a year later she gave birth to an illegitimate child whose father was a student. She is now
plagued by the thought that the student is going to leave
both her and the baby.

Charming. The customs of charming, bewitching,
enchanting, becharming, casting spells, using sympathetic
magic, conjuring and so on, are widely used as popular occult methods of curing people. And it is not just a matter of
some harmless customs being practised by unsuspecting stu-
dents of folklore, as the rationalists would suggest. Charming means treatment by magic. The practice of magic is
a matter of sorcery, even though it is at times executed in
the name of the Trinity. Sorcery utilises demonic powers
and is hence blasphemous. We need not go into the exact
nature of magic here, and a fuller account can be found in
the book *Between Christ and Satan*. However, the dangerous effects of charming can be illustrated here by means of
the following examples.

26. A young woman is a charmer. Her little boy has continually had spells cast over him as a protection against illness. By the time the boy was eight years old he started to develope a terrible temper. He used to torture animals to death or kill them by burying them alive. When he reached the age of thirteen he became a notorious drunkard. Today he drinks up to fifteen to twenty pints of wine daily. His sexual life has run wild and he has sexual relations with animals. The minister of his village traces all the defects in his character back to the charming he received from his mother.

27. A charmer from Emmental, Switzerland, ended up with a persecution mania. One January when the temperature was at minus 20° Centigrade, he ran barefoot through the village clad only in trousers and a shirt. When he was locked in a room by the other members of his family he jumped out of the window.

28. A farmer used to boast that he did not have to insure his horses as he had them regularly magically charmed. One day his son was out in a cart being pulled by four of the horses when it was hit by a train. The son and the horses were killed. The man's other two sons are both good-for-nothings and morally bad characters. The farmer himself died in a terrible fashion.

29. In a certain district a plague broke out among the cattle. A magic charmer gave the farmers some charmed pieces of paper. Stables in which these pieces of paper were kept suffered no harm. Today the village is known for its utter godlessness. It is literally under a ban. I heard of the story from the minister.

30. A man of 42 told me the following story in the course of counselling. His greatgrandfather had cured animals by casting spells over them and he had also been able to pre-

vent epidemics. He had charmed his children when they
had been ill using the name of the Trinity with some bacon
rind which he had then buried next to the house. The
prescription had always seemed to work and the children
had always got better. However, the greatgrandfather's
descendants had suffered some awful after-effects. His
children and grandchildren had all been burdened and
several of them, although wanting to become Christians,
found it impossible to do so. Some of them exhibited
mediumistic abilities including clairvoyance and cryptesthe-
sia. Others became morally depraved, and four grandchildren have very strong sexual tendencies. They want to
marry but are unable to do so. Also ghosts have been seen
in the house. The man himself who was telling me all this
also felt the curse of not being able to marry. He had been
engaged to a girl but had broken off the engagement.

31. A paralysed woman was taken to a so-called prayer
healer by her relatives. The man murmured something to
the woman which the relatives could not understand. Next
day some pus and some water came out of her ears and the
pores of her face, and she was able to walk. Her children
are all burdened. One son as well as two grandchildren
are epileptic, and although they have all expressed a desire
to become Christians they are unable to do so.

32. A minister told me that as a young boy he was sent
to a wart charmer. The charmer got rid of his warts by
some strange ceremonies. They had disappeared the next
day. The minister afterwards became mediumistic. Later
when he was studying for the ministry he heard of how
the charmer had died. A nurse who had been there at the
time said that he had died in a terrible way. He had groan-
ed and cursed and wailed for days. There had been a
terrible stench in his room and even the nurses had not
been able to bring themselves to stay in it for long. On one

occasion when the nurse returned to the room the man had died. He lay in the bed with his skull crushed in and looking completely black.

Charming creates severe oppressions. Yet through Christ deliverance is possible. "If the Son shall make you free, you shall be free indeed." The following counselling experience confirms this.

33. A 28-year-old woman came to be counselled. For five years she had been in continual pain suffering from eczema. The skin specialists could find no cause for the illness. I asked her if her family had had any contact with occultism. She said it had, explaining that her grandfather had been able to heal animals and people in the name of the Trinity. Her grandmother had also been a charmer. Two of her sisters lived dissolute lives. The woman herself was gifted with second sight and had prophetic dreams. She had once seen her brother-in-law in a dream and he had said, "I am coming home tomorrow." Sure enough, although he had been in Algeria he returned home the next day. On another occasion she had a dream in which some black hands had come towards her and some black rats had started to eat her legs. Next morning her sister came and for no reason at all began to quarrel dreadfully with her. The eczema then appeared on her legs and it proved to be incurable. The woman willingly allowed herself to be led to Christ. She confessed her sins and through faith accepted forgiveness. I prayed with her. She said next day that the terrible pains in her legs had disappeared after we had prayed together.

Christian Science. Because of its effects Christian Science belongs to the list of occult movements. The founder, Mary Baker Eddy, was originally a spiritist. She taught that death and disease could be overcome by the powers of the mind within us. But there is still no proof of this today. Every believer in Christian Science has to die, the founder included. In my counselling work my attention has been drawn in particular to their so-called practitioners. One is forced to the conclusion because of their effects that there are men in their ranks who use occult forces. People have often confessed to me that after coming out of the Christian Science movement they have been persecuted by these practitioners.

Some years ago the diary of Mary Baker Eddy was published. In it she wrote that mental powers can be used not only to heal but also to harm a person. This she called 'mal-practice'. Here we have evidence that Christian Science practitioners are able to persecute members who have left the movement.

34. A man who had been actively engaged in Christian Science realised his error and announced that he was going to leave the movement. He received a letter from the centre in Boston to the effect that he would regret this decision. Shortly afterwards he was struck down by an inexplicable illness. He shed his skin like a snake and this recurred twice and on the third occasion he died.

I have met similar cases of this in the field of magic. Charmers and healers are able to inflict diseases on people just as easily as they can heal people.

35. After many years as a member of the Christian Science movement a woman found her way to Christ and left the sect. Since then the woman has been strangely tempted. She is convinced that her former Christian Science practitioner is now using his powers against her.

36. A child of six became ill. The parents-in-law were Christian Scientists and they said to the young mother, "We'll concentrate on the child tonight. It will be alright."

Next morning at seven the mother-in-law rang up and said, "I've got the impression that the child is better." The mother could only reply, "But he died last night at twelve."

Now and then Christian Scientists publish reports that are decorated with such wonderful Christian thoughts that simple Christians are deceived by them. The *Christian Science Monitor* falls into this category, and to mention one book, there is Agnes Sandford's book *Healing Light*, which, although excellently written, is not in line with the Word of God.

Clairvoyance. Clairvoyance, clairaudience and clairsentience all belong to the list of mediumistic forces and subjections. The question of these phenomena is gone into in detail in the book *Christian Counselling and Occultism* (pages 48-64). The following are just a few examples.

37. A 6-year-old girl dreamt that the neighbour had set fire to her parent's house. When she told them the next morning they calmed her down and told her not to repeat the dream to anyone. A year later the dream came true. One night the house was burnt to the ground. After a police investigation the neighbour was convicted of the crime.

38. A woman of 44 told me the following story. Her first husband was shot by the Gestapo. She had foreseen the event four days before it happened. Her second husband was admitted into a hospital. The woman had seen an empty hospital bed and a withered hand in a dream. Next day on visiting the hospital she found that her husband's hands were cold and stiff. He died shortly after this. She is now engaged to a third man and when I counselled her she said that she had already foreseen his death.

39. A young man in a village suddenly disappeared. The relatives organised a search for him and it was thought that

he had committed suicide. The whole village took part in the search. It was without success. They then sought the advice of a crippled man from a neighbouring village. The cripple had the reputation of having some remarkable abilities. He said that the young man had been murdered and that his body was to be found in a remote part of the forest. His prediction proved to be true and they found the young man's body, severely beaten up, in the specified place.

40. There are three types of magic charmers in Alsace. First there are the 'slipper priests', then the 'urine tasters', and finally the so-called 'sleepers'. The slipper priests ask their patients to send them their slippers. Through holding the slipper in their hands they are able to name the patient's illness. The urine tasters do not analyse the urine for its albumen, sugar and haemoglobin content etc., but merely hold a sample in their hands and thus arrive at a correct diagnosis. The sleepers put themselves into a trance and by concentrating in this way are able to state the patient's illness.

41. There is a magical clairsentient who is able to diagnose illnesses with one hundred percent accuracy. A medical professor once tested his ability and discovered that the clairsentient was able to arrive at a diagnosis in next to no time even with the most difficult of cases. Ever since then the professor has sent his most problematic cases to the clairsentient for his diagnosis. The clairsentient is also able to determine from what a person has died as long as he is given some article or object which belonged to the dead person.

Colour Therapy. Colour therapy is a speciality of New Zealand. It is basically a form of radiesthesia which we have described more fully in the section on the use of a rod and pendulum. We must again say to the rationalists that this is not just a pack of lies and all a matter of fake. Healings actually do take place. Yes, it does help people — but the price is high.

All methods of healing involve the ideas of diagnosis and therapy. Well, what does this entail in the case of colour therapy? For diagnosing they use a divining rod, or a pendulum, or a mechanical pendulum called a motor skopus. The diagnosis is based upon mediumistic powers and not on the scientific background which colour therapists actually claim. We can illustrate the truth of this by quoting an example from New Zealand.

42. A colour therapist was asked by a sick man, "Can you say what a person is suffering from even when he isn't present with you?" "Yes", was the reply. "All that is needed is for the person to phone me. I just take a pendulum in my hand during the phone call and determine through the contact I have with the voice what the illness is." The man then asked, "Can you diagnose the illness of a person in another country?" "Yes. All the person need do is to send me some article, as for example a handkerchief, or some hair, and so on. I then use the pendulum over the article to diagnose the illness." This example was told me in Palmerston North.

The story indicates clearly that this was a case of mediumistic divination or clairvoyance, rather than a scientific diagnosis. This can be seen even more clearly in the statement of a very strong colour therapist who said once, "I don't need an article to diagnose the illness. I only have to concentrate in my mind on the person concerned and I immediately know what the sickness is." Of course, not all colour therapists have such strong abilities and the most common method is for a rod or a pendulum to be used over

the sick person's body, or to take the patient's hand and
use the pendulum over a box containing coloured threads.
There are many variations.

And now we come to the problem of the therapy. Most
colour therapists merely single out a coloured thread with
the pendulum and then the patient has to swing this thread
over the sick part of his body. This is supposed to speed
up certain rays or vibrations connected with the body so
as to induce healing. But not all colour therapists use such
threads. Some of them just use their own 'mental powers'
to influence the patient.

Without doubt these healings are accomplished through
suggestive or mediumistic forces. However, the Christian
counsellor is not so much interested in the medical nature
of the healing process or in the number of healings obtained
as in the question, "What is the character of these mediumistic healing powers, and what effect have they on the
patient?"

Having come across and observed mediumistic forces
for over 35 years of work as a Christian counsellor I can
say that although these forces are not to be directly equated
with the demonic, they are in fact an open door to the
devil's work. And as I have said, I have seen what these
forces can induce in a person who has contact with them,
and the evil effect they can have on one's Christian faith,
character and psychic health. For this reason I cannot warn
people too strongly against the use of colour therapy and
similar practices.

Much confusion has been caused in New Zealand through
preachers of the gospel either actively or passively using
colour therapy. Why do Christians dabble with such forces
instead of calling on the Lord for healing or for the gifts
of the Holy Spirit?

In my booklet *I Like New Zealand*, you will find more details on the subject, and in my book *Christian Counselling and Occultism*, I have gone into the scientific background of radiesthesia and the use of a rod or pendulum much more fully.

Death Magic. This brings us into the most sinister area of magic. In many places it is a common practice to pass the illnesses of the living on to the dead. One method is for a person to write the illness down on a piece of paper together with a magic charm or spell, and to throw it into the grave, or put it in the coffin of the dead person. Symbolic magic is also frequently used. The person who is ill may have a piece of their clothing or some other article put into the coffin in order to get rid of their complaint. In the book *Witches Among Us*, Kruse tells the following story: "In the town of Mehldorf just before a coffin was nailed down I was shown five coins, two small pieces of women's underwear, a piece of felt from a hat and the finger from a man's glove. After I had been shown them they were replaced in the coffin. Since it was a question of a 'better corpse', without exception the articles belonged to people who were quite well-to-do." Sometimes the dying person actually wants to take an illness of a relative with him. An example.

43. A woman lay in hospital seriously ill. She asked the nurse the following: "Nurse, will you tell my daughter to bring me one of her vests. She's been ill for years and so I want to take her illness to the grave with me when I die." The nurse did not think the request strange at all because death magic was often practised in that area. One thing to note, though, is that the accompanying article is not the decisive thing about the magical treatment. No, pride of place belongs to the magic spell repeated at the time.

Eye-Diagnosis. A furious battle is being fought today on the subject of eye-diagnosis. Eye-diagnosticians assert that they can see what a person is suffering from merely through looking at the irises. They divide the right iris into sectors and the left iris into rings claiming that each organ of the body is localised within these areas, and so implying that every type of illness can be recognised through characteristic changes produced by it in the iris fibres. First of all, though, we must point out that there are about ten different systems of eye-diagnosis. It must also be mentioned that in the medical field it is recognised that certain diseases do have a visible effect on the iris, as for example certain forms of rheumatism. Moreover, the eye's general appearance can supply one with a certain amount of useful information when diagnosing an illness. However, apart from these few factors, medical specialists dismiss the idea of eye-diagnosis. A professor of ophthalmology gave the following reply to an enquiry on this matter: "On behalf of the medical faculty I am replying to your question on eye-diagnosis. It must first of all be said that it has nothing to do with the exact sciences. We are dealing here rather with a wild conglomeration of pseudo-scientific expressions and more or less superstitiously based theories, to put it mildly. For example, some eye-diagnosticians claim that through looking at a person's eyes they can say if the patient's grandfather died from a stroke, or if the patient himself will commit suicide. Others even go as far as predicting whether the suicide will be a bloodless one or not! Starting from the anatomically based fact that each organ of the body is furnished with nerves and also with so-called 'life nerves', the eye-diagnostician maintains that each mental quality and characteristic is localised by means of sympathetic fibres in particular areas of the irises, and that a mere fleck in the iris is sufficient to prove that the patient has a poor liver, or is envious and greedy, and so on.

Eye-diagnosis can be traced back to astrology and originated in China. It has frequently been the subject of whole series of tests and has been found to be completely untenable. In the medical science of ophthalmology it is recognised that many common illnesses can be diagnosed from the state of the eyes, but in these cases the illnesses are known to effect the eyes directly. A negative result is thus no indication that the body is in a state of health, but within limits a consideration of the state of the eyes can be a help in the diagnosis. It is true that one can actually see a part of the brain tissue by looking at the optic nerve, and that the blood vessels of the eye are sufficiently exposed to allow one to see the circulation of the blood. However, this is not the same as having all the organs of the body represented in the irises." Signed: Prof. Dr. Velhagen.

This expert's opinion, however, by no means solves the problem of eye-diagnosis. The questions which face one in counselling work cannot be answered by purely medical arguments. The problem which arises when counselling a person, is not whether eye-diagnosis is of medical help or not, but whether it damages the faith of real Christians. To those who ask this question I can give certain assurances based on observations made over a considerable period of time. As far as I know some forms of eye-diagnosis are not harmful to one's faith. About six types in all fall into this catagory. If I ever come across evidence to the contrary in my counselling work I will mention it in further editions of this book. Up till now though, I see no reason to doubt that this is the case.

However, there are occult forms of eye-diagnosis which I have come across in my work, and people must be warned about them. The best way to illustrate this is by quoting a case I was faced with in Alsace, France.

44. During a week of meetings at Gebweiler a woman came to me and told me that her daughter was to die within a few days. I was astonished at this, and asked her how she knew. She explained that an eye-diagnostician from Strasbourg had prophesied that her daughter would die when she had her fifth child. And now her daughter expected her fifth child within the next few days and so it would soon be over. I told the woman that our lives are in the hands of God and that the eye-diagnostician was a false prophet subject to the wrath of God. What happened? During the mission the expected child was born, and the child's mother remained in good health. The woman returned again and complained, "You wait and see. There will be complications later." I was almost angry with her and replied, "There will only be complications if you refuse to rid yourself of your superstitious ideas." How did the story end? The young mother whose death had been prophesied is still alive today. However, although the pernicious prophecy of the eye-diagnostician failed to come true, it caused untold anxiety and concern. It was quite obviously not eye-diagnosis but fortune-telling.

Many of our healers and occult practitioners use eye-diagnosis mediumistically rather than medically. That means that they are only interested in the iris as a mediumistic contact. In this way the human eye serves a psychometric purpose in much the same way as hand lines do when a fortune-teller uses them as contact material or as an 'intuition stimulant'. When this is the case eye-diagnosis becomes a form of fortune-telling. Because of this these eye-diagnosticians are often very successful. Indeed some of them with little or no medical training can diagnose illnesses with 100% accuracy. We are touching on a problem here which, in spite of all the denials of the rationalists, still exists today. The world of the scientists in which we live is integrated with and overlaid by a mediumistic world governed by entirely different laws. The human mind fails to see any link between these two orders of nature, and the disciples of each order are for ever at war with one another. This mediumistic order of nature has already been anticipated by many people. When pantheists speak of nature possessing a soul there is a grain of truth in the idea. However, when this soul is equated with God, nature becomes an idol, and this amounts to a form of apostacy and blasphemy. When Professor Osty, Hans Driesch, and Eduard von Hartmann speak of a world soul, we have again a tiny grain of the truth. But, as we have said, if the intention is to equate this with God we are entering into idolatry.

What is the character then of this mediumistic order of nature? The New Testament states that the world is Satan's domain. By nature we find ourselves under the authority of darkness. The person who comes to Christ for salvation is delivered from this dark world's dominion. Whoever refuses to accept Christ as Lord remains under the power of Satan. Whoever of his own free will subscribes himself to the 'prince of this world', or whoever inherits a curse of this nature from his forefathers, will have the effects of the powers of darkness displayed in some way or other in his life. Mediumistic powers are not of God, even if they appear in a harmless and religious or occasionally scientific guise. This is proved a thousand times over by the effects of occult practices. Three examples in connection with occult eye-diagnosis will be used to show this.

45. A father visited a medical practitioner with his son.

The doctor used eye-diagnosis to determine the nature of the illness. He went further than this and also prophesied the son's future. After the treatment the organic disease disappeared. But there were visible changes in the young man's religious life. He discovered that he was psychically troubled whenever he wanted to go to church, and this occurred particularly during the sermon. He could no longer pray or join in singing hymns, and he lost his faith. His former frankness and honesty concerning Christianity disappeared. Instead he became subject to various passions. He started drinking and smoking excessively. He began suffering from attacks of depression and was plagued with suicidal thoughts. In the end the young man had a complete nervous breakdown and became psychically bankrupt. He had been cured of his organic complaint but instead had suffered psychical complications.

46. A mother took her eleven-year-old son to a doctor who practised eye-diagnosis. The boy later became a terrible onanist, committing masturbation twice a day. He also developed a terribly cynical attitude together with a ferocious temper, and was always quarrelling. His school work suffered accordingly and his relationship with his mother deteriorated, although previously it had been very good.

47. A mother went with her 16-year-old daughter to see a charmer and eye-diagnostician in Appenzell, Switzerland. After an eye-diagnosis the girl was treated magically. The illness vanished, but the girl's character changed drastically after the treatment. She developed a fearful temper, became sexually abnormal and started having depressions. Her sister suffered the same fate when she too was charmed by the same man. The other children who have not been charmed show no signs of being similarly burdened.

Fanaticism. Extremism and fanaticism are at present one of the greatest problems of the Christian Church. Fanatics have existed in every generation and within every Christian movement. They consist of the scum and dirt which is brought to the surface by the genuine movements. Fanaticism has also much in common with occultism. This reveals itself first of all in the effects. In extremist sects laying on of hands often has the same by-products as magic charming. The second thing that reveals this is the symptoms. The people most infected by fanaticism are those whose spiritual lives are psychically oriented or who are mediumistically inclined. The following three examples support this observation.

48. In Karlsruhe a former spiritistic medium came several times for counselling. She had severed herself from all her previous spiritistic practices and wanted to become a Christian. However, she still had to battle against her former mediumistic abilities. In the course of conversation she told me, "I've heard the three miracle healers Br., H. and Z. speak, and I got immediate mediumistic contact with each of them, although it was quickest with Br." She then added, "I don't find that I've got any contact with you." "Thank God that you can't," I replied.

I had exactly the same experience in Munich. After a meeting at which I had spoken about the dangers of occultism, a woman came up to me and told me that she too had been able to make immediate mediumistic contact with these same three healers.

49. A minister who worked in a magically infected village of Schleswig-Holstein noticed that members of his congregation who indulged in magic wandered easily into extremism. This is a significant observation and is another indication that extremism has close ties with occultism.

50. A minister from Switzerland told me the following
story. For years he had had symptoms of paralysis in his
right arm and leg. Medical treatment had produced no
improvement. He had later gone to a meeting at which
T. H. was speaking and had participated in the healing
part of the meeting. As H. was unable to pray with each
person individually he asked those who wanted healing to
stand up and place their hands on the diseased spot. He
then prayed for them. The minister did as H. had said and
afterwards felt an improvement in the condition of his
arm and leg. He had felt a tingling sensation in them and
the heaviness had literally flowed out of them through his
fingers and toes. The healing lasted from May 1955 to
December 1956. I asked the minister if he had had any
previous contact with charming in his life. He said that he
had, because on one occasion he had been succesfully charmed against warts.

The last two examples show us the close relationship
which exists between fanaticism and occultism. Occult
subjection is on the same level as a fanatical mental attitude. Whoever indulges in occultism, or whoever suffers
from his parent's or grandparents' involvement, is wide
open to fanaticism. This was the reason why I asked the
minister if he had had any previous contact with charming,
because I wanted to find out if he was mediumistic or not.
My suspicions proved to be correct. As a result of his mediumistic faculties he had felt the tingling sensation of the
disease flowing out of his finger tips. This is typical of
healing accomplished through magically based mesmerism.
In my opinion, extremist and fanatical movements often
represent occult movements, and I am not alone in this
opinion. Johannes Seitz to whom God gave many spiritual
gifts, described the extremist Pentecostal movement at the
turn of the century as the 'elite' of hell. Br. was himself

described as a medium by some Christian workers in America. Some object that Br. was not a Pentecostal but a Baptist. This is true on the surface of things, but on the whole it was the extreme forms of Pentecostalism that gave him most support. And in addition to this the German Baptists do not recognise him.

Although we shall be using the word 'pentecostal' several times in this section we must make it clear what we mean by the term. Not all Pentecostals are fanatical. One can find sound and genuine believers in Pentecostal churches. I myself have found wonderful Pentecostal believers in New Zealand and in the USA. Because of Br.'s movement some well-known leaders of the Swiss Pentecostal churches have it to their honour of having recognised that the spirit behind the movement was wrong, and have subsequently withdrawn their support from it. The evidence weighs heavily against Br. then, if his practices even became too much for some Pentecostals.

With the provision then that there are sound Pentecostal Christians, I will now give a number of experiences which I have come across in my counselling work concerning extremism and fanaticism.

51. A woman went to one of H. meetings in great pain. She stayed behind for healing. H. told those who wanted healing to stand up and hold the hands of those nearest them, so forming a chain. The woman had done this. One of H.'s co-workers had then laid hands on her. Immediately after this she had collapsed and had to remain in bed for three weeks. Since then she has suffered from depressions and a strange feeling of unrest. Her previous assurance of salvation has also completely disappeared.

52. A nurse from the deaconess house called 'Bethlehem' had the opportunity to check some of the so-called healings

of H. She said that what had happened as a result of H.'s ministry was catastrophic.

53. H. once laid hands on a boy who was cross-eyed. The parents came to me afterwards and told me that the child had been unable to sleep since then. He would just lie in his cot each night with his eyes wide open. The parents connected this strange phenomena with H.'s laying on of hands.

54. A Swiss minister went to one of H.'s meetings. H. said to those who wanted healing, "If you believe that Christ can touch you now, put your hand on the place where you want to be healed. A stream of healing will flow through you all". The minister did as H. had directed. Three weeks later he came to me for advice. Since the meeting he had been greatly troubled and for some of the time had lost his assurance of salvation. It had become quite clear to him that what had taken place was not scriptural. The effects which he himself had suffered had made him suspicious of H.'s strange healing powers.

55. A woman went to one of B.'s healing meetings in Zurich. B. said to her, "I can see a light over you. An angel is coming towards you. You will be healed". The woman had been praying throughout the healing treatment, yet afterwards there was no improvement but rather a turn for the worse. For weeks she was troubled greatly with doubts about her faith. In the end, because of a terrific feeling of despair, she came to me for counselling.

56. When B. was in Zurich once, a man who had been crippled by polio and who could not walk properly went to hear him. As B. was preaching he noticed that the interpreter was staring at him intently. At the same moment he felt the stiffness in his leg diminish. After the meeting he could lift his foot about six inches higher than before. He associated this improvement with the suggestive thoughts

he had received during the meeting. However, within three weeks the improvement had vanished again. In private discussion the man told me that he had for a long time practised Coué's method of autosuggestion. B.'s preaching, he said, had had the same effect on him as a mental impulse which, as already mentioned, lost its strength after about three weeks.

57. At another meeting B. said to the congregation, "If you believe that I am a prophet of God, say yes". A minister together with others present called out yes. After the meeting as he was driving home he fainted. He was also sick and suffered a hemorrhage. The hospital could find no reason for his strange illness. The minister then began to suffer from depressions and for weeks was inwardly disturbed. These troubles and trials of faith continued for months.

58. A minister told me the following story about one member of his congregation. A woman who had been a member of his church for years allowed a Pentecostal minister to lay hands on her. She afterwards began to have visions. She predicted that she would shortly ascend into heaven. As the supposed day approached she told her relatives to come and be with her, and she made herself ready. She washed and put on a long nightdress in preparation for her ascension, and lay in bed with an expression of great joy on her face. Her husband went and fetched the minister and asked him to put a stop to the nonsense. But when the minister had come the woman said to those present, "The Lord will come and fetch me at midnight." The appointed time drew near. The relatives were very tense, not knowing what would take place. However, the minister had all the clocks in the house which chimed the hours stopped. He told the relatives not to tell the woman the time either. When it was about half past twelve the woman said, "It

must be 12 o'clock by now." The minister replied, "It's already half past twelve!" On hearing this the woman sank back on the bed. She was utterly disappointed. Some time after this the minister talked to the pastor of the Pentecostal church about the woman. In the course of conversation the pastor said, "When people have hands laid on them and receive the baptism of the Holy Spirit it's easy for alien spirits to gain entry." The woman had indeed experienced this at her 'baptism of the Spirit' and had later been seduced by the false spirits that had crept into her life.

59. A woman was invited to a meeting at a Pentecostal church. She heard someone speaking in tongues and it clearly appeared to be a foreign language. Because she was interested she wrote down phonetically what was said. A few months later she told a missionary about this. On hearing the language he said he worked in the very area where it was spoken. On translating the message that had been spoken in tongues the woman was astonished to find that it consisted of a lot of gross blasphemy against the Trinity and immoral expressions.

60. A girl was converted. Being a young Christian she knew little about which church to join and so she got involved with an extreme Pentecostal church. When the two leaders of the church laid their hands on the girl she received some mediumistic gifts. She was able to go into a trance and thereby become a kind of medium, able to contact the world of the departed. Because in her conscious states she prayed a lot, a great discrepency developed between her prayer life and her mediumistic abilities. She began to suffer from depressions and suicidal thoughts. She was frightened at night by experiences involving ghosts. Other members of the Pentecostal church had similar experiences. In the end the girl happened to meet some genuine and sound

Christians. She realised the difference at once between these Christians and the fanatical and spiritistic Pentecostal church. She left the extreme movement and after a hard battle was completely delivered.

61. A man who had suffered from migraine for years allowed a member of a Pentecostal church to lay hands on him. The migraine disappeared immediately but he later developed a sensitivity towards the moon and certain winds. He found he was no longer able to pray, and he began to suffer from depressions and become addicted to alcohol. The Word of God just left him cold and nothing meant anything to him any more.

62. An evangelist of an extreme Pentecostal church held a mission. At the end of one of the meetings he said, "If anyone wants to receive the baptism of the Holy Spirit will you stay behind for a short after-meeting?" A number of women and girls remained behind. The evangelist told them, "There are 50 angels present here to witness the baptism of the Spirit." He then laid hands on those who had stayed behind and prayed with them. The woman telling me the story had also been there, and she went on to say that as the man laid hands on her she lost consciousness. When she woke up she found herself in a room with barred windows. She discovered from a nurse that she had been admitted into a clinic for nervous diseases three days previously. After a brief examination she was at once discharged. From then on, the woman said, she had felt as if she had been possessed. At night she began to see and to hear ghosts and shadowy figures. The neighbours and other people in the house started hearing men's voices. She described how she could not pray, and how animal cries and male voices would come out of her. As she had already been in the habit of holding Bible studies for 20 years, she

described the state she was in as possession. She was also convinced that the particular Pentecostal evangelist in question was a servant of Satan rather than a man of God. What she told me was confirmed by another confession. The evangelist had robbed one victim of £ 400 through hypnosis. He had also laid hands on the exposed breasts of both women and girls, as well as on the lower parts of their bodies, with the excuse that the whole body must be filled with the Spirit of God.

63. A woman minister of an extreme Pentecostal movement told her female followers that Christ's return was very near. At a meeting they all undressed and waited for the rapture. However, instead of Christ returning the police arrived and arrested the woman. She was sent to jail because of this.

64. A young man with cancer of the bladder heard of a Pentecostal evangelist with the gift of healing. In spite of his having little hope of being cured he went to see him. The evangelist prayed with him and then laid hands on him. Now the man was cured, so the evangelist said, and he should not doubt this under any circumstances. He was to regard whoever denied this as a servant of Satan. The patient returned and told everyone that he had been cured by the laying on of hands. A minister from his neighbourhood went to have a talk with him. However, the young man was completely deaf to all spiritual advice. The minister visited him time and time again, for the man, in spite of his healing, just lay in bed unable to get up. On his tenth visit the minister took hold of the patient and said to him, "Either you are really healed and can get up, or you've got to admit that you are still not well." It was only then that the man admitted that the pains had increased immeasurably and that he could not even move. He was finally ready to talk, and it transpired that ever since the

strange 'healing', he had experienced a terrible spiritual numbness within himself. He died the following day.

65. A Christian woman became a member of an extreme Pentecostal church. They made it clear to her that conversion and rebirth were not enough. She had to experience the baptism of the Spirit through the laying on of hands. After some hesitation the woman agreed to go through with it. After the 'baptism of the Spirit' she found herself under the special guidance of some spirits. These spirits would give her orders about how she ought to live. For example they told her not to eat pork, to abstain from marital rights and so on. Because of the leading of these spirits the woman was so plagued that she felt she could not even think for herself. She therefore decided to leave the Pentecostal church. But this was easier said than done. The spirits now became very active. They gave her no peace either day or night, and they tried everything to prevent her leaving the church. In the ensuing battle she also saw apparitions of departed people. She was finally liberated after a difficult fight. The restraint on her own mind and the spirit phenomena disappeared for good.

66. A teacher went with his wife to a very extreme Pentecostal church. The prayer meeting of the church was so turbulent that the people would work themselves up into a kind of ecstasy. They would then shout and scream and roll about on the floor. The teacher's wife was expecting a baby at the time they visited the church. During the meeting itself, while members of the church were in this state of ecstasy the expectant mother lay on the floor completely rigid. When the child was born it was found to be abnormal. However, her other five children were quite healthy. But the woman had only gone along to this fanatical Pentecostal group after the birth of the fifth child.

Although we have been giving examples of the excesses of these extreme and fanatical groups, our motive is not based on a spirit of spiteful criticism. No, the Scriptures command, "Prove the spirits to see whether they are from God." We are living in an age in which fierce wolves are threatening the Church of Christ, and they are leading many astray through their over-spiritual appearance. This is accomlished through conversation and also through the publication of various magazines and books.

To be fair, though, it is only right to mention that people are sometimes converted through the ministry of those responsible for these magazines and books. But this may only be a proof that God can even save a person through an erroneous movement. God's saving grace reaches even to the depths of hell. It can therefore be a token of the immeasurable greatness and power of the grace of God. However, through my counselling work I am sad to say that the people who have been converted by the ministry of these men tend to develope a strong personal attachment to them as well. They find it difficult to accept anything from other Christians and are unable to hear any criticism against the movement to which they are attached. Happily I know of people who have realised this, and who have subsequently withdrawn from the movement which was the means of their conversion.

A section on fanaticism and extremism could never be concluded without we ourselves crying out to God in repentance. One of the greatest needs among Christians today is caused by a lack of God's power and His gifts. Extremist movements are often just a sign of the emaciated state of the Christian Church. The most effective defence against such movements would be a movement of repentance among ourselves in conjunction with a cry to God for a genuine revival. Christ's Church must also be more alert to the nearness of the Lord's return, for it is He who will bring to an end once and for all the terrible division and confusion to be found in His Church.

Fetishes. The use of fetishes, like other occult customs, originated in heathendom. The Latin word *factitious* means magical, efficacious. A fetish can be described as an object charged with magical powers and carried about as a means of protection. Amulets, talismans and fetishes are thus very similar to one another.

The worship of relics in the Roman Catholic Church often sinks to the same level. A recent example.

67. At a lecture in Munich a research chemist gave me a relic in an envelope consisting of a small piece of cloth from a shirt. On the front of the envelope were written the words, "Ex veste P. R. Mayer S. J.", and on the back, "St. Michael JHS München (Munich)". What did it mean? In 1945 the Jesuit priest R. Mayer died in Munich after serving his church all his life. The Vatican has already received a request to make him a saint. Our desire is not to belittle the achievements of this man. However, we find it difficult to understand the Catholic Church when it issues a paper giving a list of prayers to Father Mayer which, it claims, have been answered. Who then does the Catholic Church pray to — to Christ or to Father Mayer? Are we exaggerating? Well the pamphlet we have just mentioned carries the Church's imprimatur, and it contains the words, "Father M. is the patron saint of my life", "I have prayed faithfully to F. M.", "After an urgent prayer to F. M. a bag containing money for a journey was returned", and so on. This is even more clearly illustrated in the paper entitled *"Es wird nicht still um diesen Toten"* (Though he is dead all is not quiet). On page 13 we find, "Already 600,000 photographs have been distributed, and

40,000 full biographies, 200,000 short biographies, 500,000 booklets listing answers to prayer, and over 200,000 relics have been requested." 200,000 relics! And I now have one of them: a piece of shirt. The chemist who had passed it on to me told me that the material still contained some starch. What good is this relic? Assuming that the Catholic Church only had the best of intentions, and that the relics were only meant to be tokens of remembrance, would the common people understand it in this way? There is proof that they would not. In Munich a Catholic woman gave one of these relics to a Protestant woman, advising her to lay it on any wounds or sick parts of her body. She said that they would immerdiately start being healed. We have here a case of religiously disguised fetishism. This happened in the 20th century and no one in the Protestant camp ventures to say a word against it for fear of the consequences. One must not spoil one's relationship with the great sister Church!

Firewalking. I have come across the phenomenon of firewalking in many countries. But in each place it is characterised by its own special features.

In India the firewalkers prepare themselves over a period of three months by prolonged meditation. Following this preparation they are able to walk through fire with not the slightest sign of pain on their impassive faces.

On the island of Bali the firewalkers perform under the hypnosis of the priests. They are told that a tiger is pursuing them and that the only way of escape is to run through the fire. When these firewalkers come out of their hypnotic state they show real signs of fear and are utterly exhausted.

In the Fiji islands, only the Bequa (pronounced Beng-ga) tribe has the privilege of firewalking. White stones are heated up in a fire and they become so hot that no one can get near them and they have to be moved about by means of long poles. The firewalkers' preparation in their case takes just over a day. However, when they are ready they are neither in a hypnotic nor a spiritistic trance, but instead they are laughing and joking when they walk over the stones. Their skin remains completely unmarked, although anyone else attempting the same feat would be instantly burnt to death.

In Bangkok a university professor, a personal friend of mine, was allowed to examine the soles of the feet of some firewalkers. He found no trace of burning nor even the smell of smoke on them.

What are we to say about this rather common experience in the eastern world? Is there some way of explaining the strange phenomenon of firewalking?

68. In Japan a former firewalker came to me to be counselled. He confessed to his former activities and said that he had really deceived the audience. The fire had been made on a high platform down the centre of which there had been a narrow path. Either side of this path was a fire of wood coals. The people around and below the platform had not been able to see the path through the fire. I asked this man if he thought all firewalking was faked in the same way. He replied, "No. Most of it is genuine. It is only faked sometimes for the sake of the tourists."

69. In South Africa another firewalker confessed to his occult practice. The man was an Indian who worked on a sugar plantation. He told me that he could really walk through fire. He would prepare himself for some days through fasting and meditation, abstaining from alcohol and sexual intercourse, eating only a vegetarian diet etc. I asked him if he thought the powers he possessed over

fire originated from his own subconscious mind. "That's impossible", he replied. "The devil gives this power to those who serve him." He went on to confess that when he had become a Christian he had lost his power to walk through fire.

I know that hypnosis and trance states can protect fire-walkers from the pain, but they cannot protect a person from being burnt. One day in India a young mother walked through fire with her small baby. However, she was not fully prepared for the ordeal. Her baby fell from her arms into the fire and was dead within a few seconds. Before the people could reach it its body was just burnt to ashes.

Behind the phenomenon of genuine firewalking there are demonic forces at work, and newly born Christians can feel this in the atmosphere. I therefore put the question whether or not real Christians should take part in such demonic shows.

But we have not as yet come to the end of the problem. What is the reason behind Satan giving his followers such powers? The devil is basically an imitator of God. He tries to counterfeit all the miracles and powers of the Bible. God protected the three faithful men in the midst of the fire (Dan. 3), and so Satan seeks to boast of the same power. However, with Satan it is the power of hell.

Let us rather seek the Lord who has promised, "When you walk through the fire you shall not be burned, and the flame shall not consume you" (Is. 43:2).

Satan's powers are forbidden us. It is therefore terrible when we find the nominal Christians of the Bequa tribe on the Fiji islands practising this demonic art of the prince of darkness. Our duty is instead to trust in the Lord what-ever the dangers confronting us, knowing that He is wonderfully able to deliver us from all the problems and difficulties of this life.

Fortune-Telling. I have already dealt with fortune-telling in my book *Between Christ and Satan* and so we need not go into the question very fully here. The most important areas of fortune-telling are astrology, card-laying, palmistry, using a rod and pendulum, mirror mantic, psychometry etc. A distinction has to be made between intuitive and suggestive types of fortune-telling. Fortune-telling itself has two sides to it, influence and fulfillment. Possibly 95% of all fortune-telling, or even more, can be regarded as a matter of fraud, fake and the making of money. Yet because of its suggestive character, even fraudulent fortune-telling can be dangerous. The last 5% is dependent on extrasensory powers whose ethical character is disputed both by theologians and parapsychologists. The Bible, however, is absolutely clear on this matter. Prophecy is inspired by the Holy Spirit and is of God. Fortune-telling is inspired by the spirit of Satan and is of the devil. The effects of fortune-telling speak in a language which is equally as clear. The Scriptures label fortune-telling as blasphemy. And now some examples which could be supplemented by thousands of similar cases.

71. A 42-year-old woman had often consulted astrologers and had horoscopes cast for herself in her lifetime. She finally became very depressed and tried to commit suicide twice by taking sleeping pills. She was also plagued by sudden fits of anger. During the course of being counselled she confessed the things of her past life but was still unable to really believe. She had to struggle for months in order to get peace and an assurance of salvation.

72. A well-known Christian worker accidently read a horoscope once while staying at a hotel. He usually had no

interest in astrology and only read the horoscope because he saw it referred to his birthday. One of the things he saw written was, "Anyone driving a car today must be particularly careful." When he left the hotel he noticed that he was involuntarily driving his car at a slower speed. Because of this he commented to someone later on in the day that he must already be affected by astrology.

73. A woman used to have cards laid for herself by various people and on different occasions had detailed horoscopes cast by one particular astrologer. She also bought herself letters of protection and fortune-telling letters. She began to have suicidal thoughts and she found that she was very defensive towards the things of God. A doctor of nervous diseases said she was suffering from hysteria.

74. A young woman wanted to learn how to tell fortunes. She was taught by her sister who already practised occultism. One day there was a meeting in her church. Both the sisters went to the meeting. The second sister was converted and became a Christian. Immediately after this she herself began to experience scenes of persecution at night. Invisible forces beat her until she even bled. It was this that brought her to be counselled.

74a. A girl practised fortune-telling for a number of years. In the end she developed a persistent form of eczema on both her hands. She wanted to become a Christian but just could not believe.

Is it not part of God's mercy to us that the future is veiled? If we knew everything that lay ahead of us, decisions would be impossible, initiative would be paralysed, and we would be robbed of our joy of living. The silence of God is far more merciful than the unveiling of the fortune-tellers, although they seek to do it as a service to man. And this neglects the fact that most of this so-called 'unveiling' is of a dubious nature and carries with it much oppression and many burdens.

Freemasonry. To aid me in my assessment of freemasonry I have had the following material at my disposal: the double volume work of Alfred Wulf, *Geheimbünde in alter und neuerer Zeit,* and also the book *Das Geheimnis des Freimaurers* by F. C. Endre. There is also a very informative article on freemasonry in the theological lexicon, *Religion in Geschichte und Gegenwart,* although it is rather in favour of it than against it. However, I have come by most of my material through the personal counselling of people. Hence, to be honest and objective about the matter, I must admit that counselling will have rather furnished me with examples on the negative side than on the positive side. Freemasons who are content with freemasonry do not go to people to be counselled. But this does not negate what I have to say.

The following can be said about the history and growth of freemasonry. In Europe the year 1717 can be taken as the date of birth of the first grand lodge. In London four lodges amalgamated that year. Following this in quick succession lodges were founded in Ireland, Scotland, Madrid, Calcutta and Paris. German lodges were first founded in 1738 when Frederick the Great became a member. In Western Europe today it is estimated that there are about four million freemasons.

It is impossible to include all the lodges under one heading, either organizationally or ideologically. Some of them are completely filled with the spirit of the age of enlightenment and are enemies of Christianity. Others only accept Christians into their membership. Depending on their coinage, foundation and sphere of activity, each lodge is coloured in a different shade. I know of some in which a

strong sense of friendship and 'light worship' reigns.
Without realising it I got involved with a lodge like this
in Australia. Other lodges are philanthropically and socially orientated. In Los Angeles I was told of a lodge
which finances the studies of an ordinary theological student.

I discovered in America in particular many lodges with
a certain Christian flavour. Many ministers and elders and
pastors are members of these lodges. I have often spoken
in churches where this has been the case without realising
it beforehand. In one such church were I preached there
were the symbols of freemasonry behind the altar. In the
same church one could find plaques with the inscriptions
"*Noli me tangere*" and "Roosevelt Association". I said
to the minister concerned, "If I had known that this was a
freemasons' church I wouldn't have accepted the invitation
to preach here." It is worthy of note that the Missouri
Synod of the Lutheran Church in America forbids its ministers and elders to become members of lodges.

It might be objected that the minister I have just mentioned, who was a freemason, was more tolerant than I,
because in spite of my scruples he had invited me to speak.
However, my unwillingness is supported by an observation
made by many sound and genuine Christian ministers —
that freemason churches lack any form of spiritual life.
A strange atmosphere surrounds the religious communities
whose ministers and elders are members of freemasonry.

In Europe one can find forms of freemasonry ranging
from the purely atheistic to those with Christian leanings.
I once made the acquaintance of a leading freemason who,
as a teacher in the Third Reich, had refused to stop his
teaching of religious knowledge in spite of pressure from
the National Socialist Party. He was also a church elder

in a congregation in Westphalia for a number of years. At present he is not only a regular church-goer but is also the chief burgomaster of his town.

Why then do I have various objections to masonic lodges? There are several reasons. Endre wrote in the book I have already mentioned, "A man commits a crime. He then confesses it to a priest. The priest — in God's stead — absolves him. How simple! How attractive to human nature! How wonderful to have one's sin erased by an act of God, and so to start a new life! The power to forgive sins lies within ourselves. The possibility of starting life afresh, free of past burdens, lies within our soul . . . Things written or spoken about by men are later decreed to be revelations of God."

What are we as Christians to say in reply to statements like these? In the light of the Scriptures this is blasphemy. Can we then, when someone asks our advice, approve of a person being a member of one of these lodges?

It should act as a warning to us to find that freemasons who have been truly converted to Christ have felt obliged to come out of the movement. I know a man who was once the secretary of a large lodge. When he became a Christian his conscience at once told him to resign his position and to leave the lodge. A similar example came to my notice in Sydney. After a meeting with some Christian business men, a man came and told me the following: He had been the master of a certain lodge, and it was during this time that he had become a Christian. It was clear to him that as a disciple of Christ he could no longer retain his position in the lodge. He resigned. Decisions of this nature throw a clear light on freemasonry.

The confession that weighs most heavily against freemasonry came to me by way of a daughter of the master of a lodge in Germany. She gave me her permission to publish the material as long as I mentioned neither her own name nor the name of the lodge. Her father had been persecuted by the Nazis during the time of the Third Reich. As it is known, Hitler prohibited freemasonry. Wanting to save the secret records and documents of his lodge from the hands of the Gestapo, this master of the lodge took them home and locked them up. He forbade his daughter to read any of them. He had died shortly after this. The forbidden books had thus fallen into the hands of the daughter. She had read them and was horrified by their contents. She found one section which said that members who left the movement should be killed by the other members, and there were even directions given as to how to carry this out.

I realise that in publishing these facts I put myself in a certain amount of danger. Freemasons have already on one occasion threatened to take me to court if I did not retract some of my statements about them. I would like to make it quite clear therefore that I do know that quite a number of lodges exist which give no such directives about ex-members. I also cannot prove that the information given me concerning the contents of the books I have just mentioned is correct. However, I can confirm on oath that what I have written is a true account of what was confessed to me by the freemason's daughter in a private counselling session. And the daughter is still alive today and so could repeat her testimony at any time.

A further reason why I am strongly opposed to many lodges is the accepted use of many occult customs and rites in their practices. Again it must be repeated that some lodges do not in fact use anything occult in their ritual. However, a lot of lodges zealously indulge in spiritistic and magical rites. It is well known that certain practices of the so-called Rosecrucians have been accepted into the symbolism and customs of many lodges. But Rosecrucians indulge in a spiritistical form of spiritualism. I know this also through my counselling work. It occasionally happens that the Word of God strikes home at the conscience of a freemason and so the veil of secrecy surrounding his lodge is lifted a little at the time of his confession.

Perhaps as a last example I can mention the intellectual lodge in Zurich. I am not sure if this lodge is connected in any way with the grand Alpine lodge of Switzerland. Probably not. But whatever the case it still exists under the name of a lodge. It arranges services at which hymns are sung, the Bible is read, and prayers are said. The sermons themselves are supposed to be preached by a spirit named Joseph who speaks through a woman medium named Beatrice. This means we are dealing with a form of spiritualism with a spiritistic background.

I have been advised by well meaning people to be more tolerant towards trends like this. What am I to say? When I see one of my children making a mistake and putting a bottle of arsenic to its mouth, I must at once snatch the bottle away from the child. In the same way, am I just to stand back and do nothing while people are suffering spiritually as they come into contact with such dangerous movements? Is it not my duty as a Christian to warn people against trends like this? Am I being intolerant? Do we really need the so-called spirit of Joseph to come to us from the place of the departed? Has not Christ given us all that we need both for this life and for the world to come, for both time and eternity? It is not the light of error that we follow, for we have Jesus, the Light of the world (John 8:12).

Ghosts. As is true of all mediumistic phenomena the subject of ghosts is very debatable. A distinction has to be made between ghosts associated with people, which are subjective rather than objective and which are really a sign of illness or defect, and ghosts associated with particular places, which have been witnessed for years or even centuries by many people. As always we are up against the unconvinced and hard of hearing rationalists who seek to explain away everything by saying that it is either humbug or explicable by natural means. But at the same time one can meet the 'believing' occultists who accept anything, no matter how absurd, just at its face value. One must encourage both sides to be more objective. There is one book I can mention called *Ghosts* by Fanny Moser with a foreward by Prof. Jung of Zurich. This book goes into the question of ghosts from the scientific point of view. My own counselling work has often brought me face to face with this puzzling subject, and I have invariably found that the problem is always associated with the past or present practice of occultism in the house concerned. I have also had the opportunity of actually visiting so-called haunted houses myself. Now a few examples.

75. A Christian social worker repeatedly saw a hideous figure in her room at nights. The figure once molested her. In her anger she threw her slipper at the shadowy figure. At that instant an angel with a sinister face appeared at the end of her bed. The woman was petrified of the angel. This brings us to an important point. Having heard so many experiences similar to this in my counselling work it is possible to say that the measure as to whether the angelic vision is of God or of Satan, is whether or not the experience of the person involved is one of joy or of terrible fear. However, most visions of this nature cannot

have any real objective importance attached to them. They are far more likely to be hallucinations caused through illness, or eidetic visions, rather than genuine phenomena.

76. An elderly woman came to be counselled. She told of strange ghost-like phenomena in her house. During the night dogs would run about her room and they would try to lick her. Invisible hands used to lift her bed up, and she sometimes noticed several figures in the room. Whenever she prayed the phenomena all disappeared at once. But the haunting carried on for years although the woman was completely healthy mentally. She has neither suffered from depressions nor from any kind of mental illness. In answer to the question whether she had ever been involved with occultism she said that as a girl, both when she had been suffering from diphtheria and later with another illness, she had been healed through black magic.

77. Uli Ruppeiner from Herisau was asked to visit a woman living in Toggenburg, Switzerland. He went to see her and discovered the following. The woman's husband had hanged himself in one of the rooms. Since his burial, stamping, whistling and grinding noises had been heard in the room. The local minister who she had first consulted said that the noises were not real but due to overstrained nerves. Uli listened to the woman's story and then went into the room concerned and prayed that through Christ the haunting would cease. The noises never reappeared. So, whether the phenomenon was real or whether it was only a sign that the woman herself was ill, in either case Christ's victory was clearly visible.

78. For several generations a white figure was seen at night in a certain manse. Whenever the figure appeared it was accompanied by a lot of noise and commotion. Heavy blows like those from an axe crashed against the

door. There was not a minister whose family could stay in the house for very long. However, one minister had the courage to challenge the ghost. It turned out that whenever he commanded the ghost in the name of Christ it disappeared together with the noises.

79. At a ministers' conference once, a Lutheran minister recounted how, in two houses of his parish, for three days, stones had flown about in an inexplicable manner. The stones would come in through the windows, but instead of shattering them they left holes like those caused by bullets. And the stones always felt hot. A fire was caused by one of these hot stones on the third day. The owner of one of the houses informed the police, but the subsequent investigation proved nothing. The invisible stone-thrower remained undiscovered.

80. Some loud knocking noises were heard in a house at night. The family living there tried unsuccessfully for a long time to discover the cause and then informed the police. They in turn kept a watch on the house each night and thereby verified what the family had reported. I was able to see the police report myself. However, neither the family concerned nor the police paid any attention to the possible connection between the noises and the occult; yet as it happened, there was a man living in the house who had been charmed magically against an illness.

81. Two flat owners took each other to court. Each night loud knocking noises had been heard in the building. The people in the flat above had accused those below of the disturbance, and vice versa. The people in the lower flat asked a Christian woman to help them and just to sleep in the flat. Each time she did so she asked God to protect her, and on each occasion there were no noises to be heard. I heard of an example almost exactly the same as this from

Switzerland. Again two flat owners had accused one another and so two police officers had kept watch, one in the flat below and one in the flat above. Both of them heard the same knocking noises but neither could determine their origin.

82. A house had been haunted for years. Some Christian friends of the family advised them to look through the house to see if there was any occult literature there. The search proved to be successful. One of the servants possessed and read the 6th and 7th Book of Moses. They at once burnt the book. The haunting immediately stopped.

83. A friend of mine, a Christian worker, told me of an experience he had had as a young man at his parent's home. One day quite suddenly and inexplicably the house began to be haunted. Knocking was heard in the walls and at night they would hear heavy footsteps about the house and other sounds. As the poltergeists persisted in their game the father called in a Christian man to help them. The man prayed in each room of the house commanding the spirits in the name of Jesus to leave. The haunting immediately ceased. However, this was paralleled by another remarkable event. Almost immediately after the exorcism two of the pigs owned by the family developed a kind of rabies. They started running around their sties making a terrible noise. After watching them behave in this mad way for a couple of hours the father had no alternative but to have them both killed.

For anyone wishing to assess these cases from a psychiatric point of view, we must make it quite clear that these experiences are not those of schizophrenics or mentally ill people. In some of the cases even the police could verify that the phenomena were genuine. I could add a further example from Kiel in which eight policemen and two min-

isters were all involved in the investigation at the same
time. Every one of these ten men observed the haunting
phenomena. It is also important to note that whenever a
person prayed in the name of Christ the phenomena disappeared at once. We can learn something about their character from this. When schizophrenics hear voices and noises,
the sounds do not go away just because a person calls on
Christ.

To conclude this list of ghost stories we will mention a
wonderful case of deliverance.

84. Two men, a father and his son, came to see me and
told me that there was something amiss at their house. Each
night between 11 and 12 o'clock the whole family was disturbed by ghost-like phenomena. They were awakened by
noises and footsteps. The mother and daughter felt as if
they were being strangled. Some of the family at times
felt their faces being stroked, and they were all paralysed
with fear. They tried everything to get rid of the phenomena. They called in a Catholic priest; but, although they
followed his advice of repeating the names of the Trinity
and using three crosses, three candles and some holy water,
nothing happened. They then tried different magicians.
One of these magicians advised the family to spread a black
cloth out over three candles and then to burn the cloth,
again while repeating the names of the Trinity. Another
thing they were told to do was to put three matches under
their pillows repeating the same thing as before. Next they
were told to secure the doors and windows by means of two
knives in the form of a cross. But none of these magical
practices helped either. Someone else told them to stick
two nails crosswise through an onion and then place it
under the bed, but this too failed. The family continued
to be plagued as before. Since the two men telling me the
story appeared to be quite normal and healthy, I concen-

trated my questions on the occult side of the problem. The following facts came to light. The family had had fifteen books on sorcery in the house for many years. They had also consulted two dangerous magicians in the past. They regularly sought the help of fortune-tellers and magic charmers. Last but not least, there was a woman in the neighbourhood who practised black magic using what is called 'the Spiritual Shield'. Hence the counselling session revealed that it was a case of involvement in occultism. I told the two men that they had chosen the wrong course in seeking the help of white magic practitioners. However, I went on to tell them the way of deliverance through Christ. Since I had to leave the town shortly after this, I gave the details of our conversation to a minister, who I asked to look after the family. I later heard that they had all given their lives over to Christ, and that the ghost-like phenomena had stopped straight away.

Heresies. The army of heresies about us today is almost too large to number. To name but a few of those I have come across in my ministry we have: Anthroposophy, the Bahai world religion, Christadelphians, Christian Science, Grail worshipers, followers of Herbert W. Armstrong, disciples of Jacob Lorber, Jehovah's Witnesses, Masdasnan, Modern Theology, Mormons, the New Apostolic Church, Spiritualism, Subud, Theosophy and many others. These sects are characterized by gross fanaticism and unscriptural teaching. But as Christians we ought to be shamed and brought to a place of repentance through the strong sense of unity and the mutual sharing of responsibility one finds among members of these sects. However, to show the extent to which evil spiritual forces can be at work in these sects I will quote an example involving the New Apostolic Church in Germany.

85. A member of the New Apostolic Church came to my mother-in-law with the following tale. "Your husband appeared to us from the dead and asked to be confirmed as a member of our church. He also said that he wants all his relatives to become members as well." My mother-in-law said in reply to this, "When my husband was alive he was a sound and balanced Christian. What you have told me is utterly unimaginable. My husband has never had anything to do with heresy."

Think of the extent to which this movement went in its deceit. It staged an appearance from the dead in order to try and ensnare people. And besides this, confirmation of the dead is no more than gross spiritism. I have come up against other experiences similar to this in my counselling work. These appearances of the departed are merely an effective publicity stunt for the New Apostolic Church.

The most confusing heresy of all is Modern Theology. In the western world this theology is called new rationalistic theology. Its followers claim that Christians can only accept what their intellects can grasp. It follows that we should therefore deny that Jesus is the Son of God and that he is our redeemer. They also disbelieve in the resurrection and the second coming of Christ. They deny the existence of miracles, answers to prayer, the devil, demons, and even the personal existence of God. We can only ask, what still remains of the Bible?

But there is an even more terrible developement in this modern form of theology. The devil has learned a little about how to trap believers. Today, theologians once more use the old words as for example 'the cross', 'forgiveness', 'new birth' and so on, but they empty these words of their original meaning and fill them with new rationalistic ideas.

Though I may pray for these poor modern men and wish

for their well-being I may still see the look of dismay in their eyes when in eternity they recognise that the old-fashioned Bible is fulfilled to the very letter. How wonderful that our faith is based upon the God of the Bible and not on the ideas of these impoverished theologians.

Hypnosis. The use of hypnosis and suggestion is not confined to the psychologists and others in the medical profession, but is also practised by laymen and charlatans alike. The medical profession uses hypnosis both for diagnosis and for therapy. Dr. Lechler, a Christian psychiatrist well respected in Christian circles on the continent, believes, however, that one can only justify the use of hypnosis in diagnosis, i.e. in determining the illness of the patient. Dr. Paul Tournier, a famous doctor in Geneva goes further and states that every form of hypnosis is an invasion into the personality of man. But as we have said, other specialists use hypnosis in the course of their treatment and therapy. Yet our concern at the moment is not with the professional use of hypnosis. Our main aim is to show by means of a few examples the dangers involved when hypnosis and suggestion are used by magic charmers and unqualified medical practitioners.

86. A minister told me about the following counselling experience he had. He was called to see a member of his congregation who was sick. The woman told him that she would die within a few days. This had been prophesied by a fortune-teller. The minister attempted to disillusion her. He promised to stay with her on the day in question if she wanted him to. The doctor could find nothing physically wrong with the woman. The minister visited the woman several times endeavouring to be of some encouragement to her. The day came and nothing happened. She was all right.

87. Whenever someone in the family was ill the mother used to visit a woman who would pray them well again. This woman would make the sign of a cross over the patient three times and then stroke the diseased spot the same number of times. The patient always recovered. The mother once went to see a magician from Appenzell, Switzerland, who said to her that he would be able to influence her in such a way that she would not be able to find her way home. And this is exactly what happened. She wandered about for hours looking for the road in which she lived. During the night she was awakened by the grip of an ice-cold hand. She noticed a small man in the room with a beard and piercing eyes. The woman had herself been magically charmed and she died in a terrible fashion. All her children are abnormal. The son is an evil tempered, sexually licentious man, and he has now been admitted to a psychiatric clinic as a schizophrenic. The daughter has the same temperament as her brother.

The following two examples show the suggestive influence of films and even school lessons.

88. A mother was in tears when she told me that her young son had killed himself after coming home from the pictures. He had seen a cowboy film and at home had copied the methods of tying a person up that he had watched on the film.

89. The mother of a 14-year-old boy told me in a counselling session that her son had heard about the time of the German revolution at a lesson in school. The teacher had described the various ways in which people had been hanged. The boy had come home and killed himself while trying out the different methods.

Now and again transference can take place when a doctor uses hypnosis. This too can be dangerous. The next example illustrates this.

90. A Christian told me of an experience she had had with her mother. The mother had suffered from severe colic due to gall-stones. Once when she was in pain the family doctor was called. Instead of giving her a pain-relieving injection he hypnotised her and the pain left within a few minutes. However, after this hypnotic treatment the mother's character altered completely. She developed such an evil temper that at times it bordered on madness. She would sometimes throw plates at the wall in these fits of temper. Once she tore the electric light fittings down from the wall. Her children who have all grown up now are strongly opposed to hypnosis as a form of treatment.

This is not just one isolated case. Transferences of this nature have often been confessed to me in the course of my counselling work.

Letters of Protection. Magic letters, lucky letters and letters of protection etc., in spite of their religious exterior belong to the domain of superstition and sorcery.

91. A woman told me in a counselling session that every Sunday her father had held prayers with the family. After the Bible reading he had always read aloud from a letter, yellow with age and kept between the pages of his own Bible. One day the family read Modersohn's book *Im Banne des Teufels* (Under the Spell of the Devil), and they realised the terrible nature of the letter. Without their father's knowledge they burnt the letter. On discovering this the father was furious and beat them all. However, they felt much better after the burning of the letter because till then they had felt that there had been something wrong in the family.

92. A minister speaking at a conference related the following story. "A church elder living in a district near Wurzburg asked if he could show me a 'fire blessing'. We went and visited the owner of a large old farm house and we were led into the large barn by this farmer. There, in a compartment in the huge main beam, was the fire blessing. It was an old yellow sheet of paper on which were the words, "Anno 1645, 24 August. In the name of the Father, Son and Holy Ghost I, Satan, protect this house from lightening and fire. Signed . . . (illegible)." — The farmer was persuaded to part with this 'devil blessing', and it was later sent to the criminal investigation office in Munich for chemical analysis. The report confirmed the fact that the paper was about three hundred years old and added that the signature was written in a mixture of animal and human blood. It was about 5 o'clock in the afternoon when the fire blessing was removed from the barn. Within three hours a storm had developed and the farm house was struck by lightening. The whole place, including the barn, the cattle and the equipment, was completely destroyed. Only the people living there survived. Coincidence? The buildings were situated about a hundred yards away from the main Wurzburg-Rothenburg railway line. During the last war a munitions train had blown up in the immediate neighbourhood. Not one pane of glass on the farm had been broken. When Germany had collapsed in 1945, the S.S. had made this particular farm their headquarters and a lot of fighting had taken place around it. Again the buildings had been completely untouched. The same had happened in previous centuries. When the French had been fighting in the area of Ansbach-Bayreuth the farm had also survived. Still just coincidence? And now, what of the date, the 24th of August? It was on the 24th August in 79 A.D. that Pompey and Herculaneum were destroyed by Vesu-

vius exploding. On the night of St. Bartholemew, 24th
August 1572, tens of thousands of Huguenots including old
men, women and children were slaughtered. The fire blessing's date obviously seems to indicate a particularly effective charm. Then there is the question of the farmer's
reaction to his loss. Since the buildings had been insured
he was covered against fire and so he had them rebuilt.
But when the church elder visited him again the farmer
embraced him and said, "I am really grateful. The pressure
has lifted." The spell had been broken; the farmer had
realised it was better to lose everything than to remain in
league with the devil. But who really destroyed the buildings, Satan or God? In Job chapter 1 it says that Satan
was given permission to send down the 'fire of God' from
heaven. It is evident that Satan as the fallen prince of the
angels (Jude 6) is temporarily able, or is permitted by God,
to have access to the divine control levers of this world.
One wonders about the history and fate of the people connected with this particular farm house. Whoever disregards
the strict limits of God's laws, and thereby indulges in the
abominations and sins of sorcery must pay the price of
suffering serious psychic injuries. Satan may indeed give a
form of 'protection' or 'success' which can falsely be described as a 'blessing', but at what a dreadful cost! It could
well be that after the removal of the fire blessing Satan
vented his rage. Job 2:6, 2 Cor. 12:8 and Matt. 1:28
supply us with much food for thought. However, the
children of God can withstand all the powers of darkness
with complete faith and confidence. They need only stand
firm in the whole armour of God, wearing the breastplate
of righteousness and the helmet of salvation (Eph. 6).

Magical Healing Methods. Magical healing
methods are dealt with partly under the heading Charming,

and partly under the heading Black and White Magic. Such methods of healing do not belong to the realms of science, lying as they do outside the domain of the reason. Magic, as we have already said, belongs to the mediumistic order of nature. Here a completely different set of rules holds true. Magical healing is far more widely spread than is commonly realised. A minister in Germany told me that in his own church there were only about ten families altogether who had not practised magic in some form or another. At a ministers' conference a doctor said that where he worked in Lüneburger Heath, there was not one family in which magical healing was not practised. A Swiss minister told me that in every house at his village the 6th and 7th Book of Moses (a book on black magic) was used. For examples of this see the sections on Charming and Black and White Magic.

Mental Suggestion. Mental suggestion is a grim chapter of magic. I have gone into the question a little in my book *Christian Counselling and Occultism* (page 118), and so I will merely mention a few new examples which demonstrate the grave effects of treatment by mental suggestion.

93. A man suffering from tuberculosis of the lungs went to see a specialist. The X-rays showed a cavity in his lungs about the size of a hen's egg. The patient was at once transferred to a hospital at Davos, Switzerland. The doctor told the man's wife that the case was hopeless. His mother therefore went to an occult practitioner at Maria Einsiedel called Grätzer. For a considerable sum of money Grätzer agreed to treat the patient by means of mental suggestion. Contrary to the expectation of the doctors and indeed the patient himself, the treatment was a complete success. From the time of the healing, though, both the

religious attitude and the character of the patient altered. He stopped going to church and cut himself off from religious matters. He plunged into a life of pleasure seeking, vice and free sexual expression. He also began having suicidal thoughts. His psychical and nervous disturbances finally led him to seek counselling help. But every time he was asked to pray his concentration and his memory failed him. He always felt far away. This feeling of being distant and far away which is sometimes brought on by prayer is a symptom that the person has been magically charmed.

94. In some areas of Switzerland many of the doctors send their most serious cases to people practising mental suggestion. A minister who regularly visits patients in St. G. Hospital said once, "Patients who have accepted treatment by mental suggestion refuse to be encouraged by the Word of God. They are both insensible and opposed to the things of God."

95. A young man of nineteen developed eczema. He went to a healer who used both mental suggestion and black magic. After being treated by mental suggestion the rash at once disappeared. However, the patient's inner attitude changed immediately after this. He had previously read his Bible and prayed regularly. But now he became depressed and lost all his desire to read and pray.

Mental suggestion is the demonic counterpart to the intercessory prayer of a Christian. Anyone closely related to Christ through prayers and answers to prayer will readily understand Satan's duplicity. The devil, too, waits on his adherents for as long as God permits.

Mesmerism. Mesmerism and magnetism are a source of as much discussion as are other occult practices. On the whole doctors and scientists reject its validity. However, occultists support its use. My own pastoral work has

shown me that mesmerism is genuinely connected with
magic. It is a power belonging to the mediumistic order of
nature. I have discovered that this ability occurs in families
whose forefathers have practised occultism and in particular, magic charming. In the same way as we find the
New Testament talking about charismata, or gifts of the
Holy Spirit (1 Cor. 12:9—10), so too, there exist demonic
gifts which are, as it were, the charismata of the devil. The
decendants of charmers exhibit the following abilities:
clairsentience, second sight, heightened sensitivity, heightened suggestibility, telepathy, mesmerism, the ability to use
a rod or pendulum, the ability to go into a trance, astral-
travelling and so on. In the case of the decendants, the
magic practices of the ancestors may be curtailed, but the
resultant gifts may still remain. These gifts can indeed
diminish, and in some cases be apparently neutralised,
but they forever carry with themselves the characteristic
odour of magic. The best course of action for a person in
this position is to cease exercising the gift they have, and
to avoid the temptation of pride. Indeed people with
mediumistic gifts should ask Christ to take them away.
But now some characteristic examples.

96. A woman went to Dr. Tr. in Munich. He treated her
successfully for lumbago. During the course of the treatment she had to hold her fingers up in the air to act as
antennae for cosmic forces, or so he said. When she returned home, although she had been organically healed, from
then on her faith was hampered. She could no longer pray,
and she felt as if there was an impenetrable wall between
herself and God.

97. A Christian friend of mine who is a teacher allowed
himself to be treated by a mesmeriser. The mesmeriser was
himself reputed to be a Christian, otherwise my friend
would not have visited him. Just to be safe the teacher asked

the man, "You don't use demonic forces, do you?" The mesmeriser replied, "But demonic forces are good! Demons can help us." The patient discontinued the treatment on hearing this.

98. A mesmeriser was able to cure many kinds of diseases. His father before him had been able to ban diseases and to charm animals.

99. A Christian doctor and healer when asked about his ability to heal said, "Natural mesmerism is sufficient for about two patients daily. Whoever treats more than two patients every day either achieves nothing or is plugged in to the devil."

100. Another of my friends, an evangelical minister, told me of his experience with a certain mesmeriser. The mesmeriser had had some remarkably successful cases of healing over the years. My friend actually witnessed the healing of a girl who had been crippled from birth. The mesmeriser had healed her through magnetically stroking the illness away. When the minister and his son were both taken ill he resolved to consult the same mesmeriser. He first asked the man, "Is your gift a gift of God?" The man replied that it was. The minister therefore allowed both himself and his son to be treated. The mesmeriser did not touch either of the patients but merely made stroking movements along their spines at a distance of about six inches. While this was going on the minister silently prayed, "Lord, if this man's power is from you then bless his efforts, but if it is not from you then protect us both." After the treatment there were no signs of improvement. A few days later they went for a further session with the man but he refused to treat them saying, "You've got a different spirit." The minister now knew what he was up against and he dispensed forever with such treatment.

Pastor Modersohn, in the light of his great knowledge of occult healing methods, said, "90% of all healers, mesmerisers and magnetisers use demonic and occult powers. One must be absolutely certain with whom one is dealing before accepting treatment from such men. A person must not be blinded by the religious trimmings."

Modern Theology (see under Heresies, 20, and Neo-Rationalism, 28).

Moon-Mancy. Moon-mancy is associated with many of the superstitious and heathenistic customs of the world. For example, in some places one is not supposed to get married if the moon is on the wane. Elsewhere farmers plan their sowing according to whether or not the moon is waxing. The night of the full moon is often chosen for casting spells. Some healers charm their homeopathic remedies on the same night. I do not say this to belittle homeopathy. However, anything charmed at the time of the full moon has the same effect as magic itself. In villages where a belief in witches still exists, witch hunts are carried out when the moon is waning. The following are two examples in which sorcery and healing are connected with the moon.

101. A woman was visited by a pendulum practitioner. He sold her some tea telling her to drink a cup a day while the moon was waxing, and three cups a day when the moon was waning. She did this and her complaints disappeared, though in this case, probably more through auto-suggestion than by magic. The woman afterwards starting having depressions, a thing she had never suffered from before.

102. As a young girl a woman was charmed against an illness on a night of the full moon. She afterwards became mediumistic, and developed telepathic and clairvoyant abilities. Some insurmountable difficulties also appeared in her religious life.

Neo-Rationalism. An excellent paperback which sheds a lot of light on the roots of modern theology, and which in turn defends the Bible against the undermining influence of liberalism, is *Alarm um die Bibel* by Dr. Bergmann. For those who wish to go deeper into the subject I can also recommend the two books *Glauben an Jesus* by Prof. Künneth, and *Um die Wahrheit der Heiligen Schrift* by Otto Rodenberg.

Speaking personally, it has mainly been through counselling people that my eyes have been opened to the tragedy and burning needs associated with the modern theology and neo-rationalism about today. Jesus said, "By their fruits you shall know them" (Matt. 7:16).

A letter recently reached me from a Christian family living in the Black Forest. The writer, together with his wife and parents, is a member of an evangelical group of Christians. The letter was about his oldest boy. This son had been at the top of his class in the high school for seven years. He had been converted at a mission and had since then regularly read his Bible and prayed each morning. Then a minister had arrived in the neighbourhood. The man was a Doctor of Theology, and he took over the religious instruction of the senior form at the school. The boy who already had thoughts of studying theology was now exposed to the rationalistic theology of the new minister. The sediment deposited during the school lessons reappeared in discussions at home. The father listened anxiously as he was told: the Bible is not the Word of God, it is the work of men and contains many mistakes. The historicity of the birth of Christ and of the cross is of no consequence; the only thing that matters is the meaning behind it. The son was exposed to the opinions of the new religious teacher for two years, and gradually their destructive effects took place. Away went his thoughts of studying theology. Away went his habit of Bible reading. Away went his prayer life: allegedly there were no answers to prayer, and in the final analysis, or so he was told, prayer was only a way of easing one's mind and not a conversation with a personal 'Thou'. By now the father was justifiably asking the question, "Do we have to expose our children to the influence of teachers and ministers like this who destroy everything taught to them previously by either ourselves or genuine evangelists?" This Christian brother is extremely troubled about the fact that his younger son is now at the same school being taught by the same religious teacher.

I wrote in reply to his letter that as a father myself I have a responsibility before God to guard my children against the destructive influence of neo-rationalism. Being a minister of the established church it is better for me as a witness to refuse to let my children attend the religious lessons than to expose them to the poisonous vapours of today's destructive Bible criticism. When my own daughter was faced with a similar situation at her school, I stopped her from going to the religious lessons. Her first thoughts were, "But what will the people think if I don't go to the lessons? My father is a minister!" I told her, "I'm not afraid of what the people will say. It's a matter of what the Truth is and not of being in submission to man."

It would take too long to go into all the experiences I have had over the years relating to modern theology. Perhaps I can tell you of something I heard said in Australia. I was at a ministers' conference when some members of the Lutheran Church came and said to me, "For 400 years Germany has lead the field in theology, but for some years now our reaction to the theology originating from there is just one of horror." I have heard remarks similar to this both in East Asia and South Africa. Where are we heading when church newspapers say that Luther and Jesus only believed in the devil because they were limited to the ideas of their day. If this were true none of their statements can be authoritative. When I actually read this myself I cancelled the newspaper. Yet a protest of this nature is just a drop in the bucket. But does that matter? We ourselves must not be found guilty of a silent form of consent or toleration. Anyone attempting to explain the devil and the demons away is employed in the devil's own business. There could be nothing better for him than that he be vapourised into a vague notion of the Middle Ages which today has to be done away with.

Now an encouraging story to end with. While engaged in a mission in northern Germany a minister friend of mine told me the following story at his home. In his Christmas sermon a young minister had denied that the Christ-child was the Son of God. The elders met together after the service and after a long discussion decided not to allow theology of this nature to be preached from their pulpit. They had then told the nonplussed minister of their decision and said that he would not be allowed to speak in their church again. The church authorities were also notified to this effect and they complied with the decision. The minister was at once transfered to another post. There was quite naturally a scandal about the whole affair, but the elders are to be congratulated on their action. Would to God that every one of our congregations would come of age before the whole of Christendom becomes bedecked in a huge shroud.

Neo-rationalism means that human reason takes pride of place. Yet in the New Testament it is just this throne of human knowledge and wisdom that is overthrown. Paul writes, "Has not God made foolish the wisdom of the world?" (1 Cor. 1:20), and, "He catches the wise in their own craftiness" (1 Cor. 3:19). The Bible's answer to mod-

ern theological rationalism is, "In Christ are hid all the
treasures of wisdom and knowledge" (Col. 2:3). (See also
Heresies, 20).

Numerical Symbolism. Numerical symbolism
is a complicated labyrinth from which people with a superstitious nature are unable to free themselves. The best
known example of this is the idea that the number 13 is
unlucky. There are many hotels with no room number 13.
When I was a student at Heidelberg I used to live in one
of the halls of residence in a room numbered 12a. On
either side of my room were those numbered 12 and 14.
And this in the shadow of the university! But now the
story of a Lutheran minister with whom I once even held
some special meetings.

103. This minister was invited to a christening celebration
by a friend of his who was a doctor. After the christening
the minister was shown into the doctor's dining room. He
became very agitated when he saw how many places had
been set for dinner. He got up quickly and said to his old
school friend, "I can't sit here. The table has been set for
thirteen people. It won't be good." The doctor was surprised and replied, "How can you, a minister, say that? You
are supposed to bring people out of superstition." A lively
discussion developed and it was even humourous, but the
minister was serious, and he stood his ground. In the end
it was decided that the children would have their meal in
the room next door so that there would no longer be thirteen people at the table. Three months later the minister's
youngest child died. The doctor went to the funeral. On
the way back from the cemetry they mentioned the occasion of the christening. The doctor again sought to resist
the minister's superstitious ideas. That same night the doctor's own child became seriously ill and by the next morn-

ing it had died. When the child had been buried the minister asked the doctor, "Do you now believe that 13 is an unlucky number?"

What agreement is there between the Christian message that the minister had to preach and this rank superstition?

Everyday life is filled with this strange symbology regarding numbers. It is supposed to be unlucky to buy raffle tickets on the 13th day of the month. One should not sow an even number of beans together. An odd number of chicks get on better than an even number. It is unlucky for a ship to sail on the 13th day of the month. To be the third person to light a cigarette from a match is considered to be unlucky. To put three crosses over a doorway or window is thought to be lucky. And so we could go on. It would be better for us to turn our eyes away from these superstitious ideas and instead to ask the Lord to teach us "to number our days that we may get a heart of wisdom" (Psalm 90:12).

Occult Literature. Occult literature drifts among the people like a great cloud of poisonous gas. It poisons the minds and the souls of those who read it. One has, to mention but a few titles, *The 6th and 7th Book of Moses*, *The Book of Venus*, *The Other Side*, *The Greater World*, *The Psychic News*, and the psuedo-Christian works of Jacob Lorber and other such authors. It is tragic to relate that the dangerous book on magic *The 6th and 7th Book of Moses* is still being printed and distributed today by a publisher in Brunswick, Germany. Several court cases have been held in an attempt to prohibit the publishing of the book but all to no avail. There are still loopholes in our laws which make it impossible to prevent the distribution of such devilish merchandise. If a person wants more information on this subject it is

recommended they read the appropriate section in my
book, *Between Christ and Satan*. One thing that must be
made absolutely clear though, is that one should never
keep books on occultism in the house. It is not even safe
to keep referring to these books for the sake of study or
some other educational purpose. I have often heard it
said by a wife, "Since my husband brought the 6th and
7th Book of Moses into our home to study it, there has been
nothing but unhappiness, quarrelling and discord in our
family."

Here is just one example involving some spiritistic literature.

104. A woman used to read whatever spiritistic and spir-
itualistic literature that came her way. The messages of the
medium called Beatrix from the intellectual lodge of Zurich were her substitute for regular church attendence. The
writings of the mystic Eckhart and the spiritistic medium
Jacob Lorber replaced the apostolic Scriptures. The central
idea of her religious beliefs was that man should strive to
reach a form of God-consciousness within himself. Sin and
salvation played no part in her thinking. Man is basically
good and needs only to evolve to a higher plane. The
'godly spark' within all men must be fanned into a flame.

The writings of the excommunicated apostate priest Johann Greber can also be included under a heading of occult
literature. He actually translated the whole of the New
Testament in a spiritistical sense.

Omens. There are many signs and omens which
are supposed to be of importance in our everyday lives,
determining and influencing what we do. We will begin
with some examples.

105. An 80-year-old church elder told me the following
story. His wife had died 25 years ago. However, they had

been warned beforehand that this would happen. When I asked him about the nature of the warning he told me that in the spring of that year a root had grown straight out of the ground in their garden. He said that this was always a sign that there would be a death in the family. In spite of my telling the man that this was shear superstition he remained adamant.

106. A woman said that one night three clocks in the house had stopped. Because of this she had known that someone in the family was about to die. However, in this instance nothing happened.

The following signs are supposed to herald good luck: horse shoes, toad stools, piglets, four-leafed clover, ladybirds, forget-me-not, mistletoe at Christmas, a cobweb in the room, yew trees, money spiders, a sprig of heather, two shooting stars in one night and so on. There are also the proverbs like, "See a pin and pick it up, all the day you will have good luck", and, "Something old, something new, something borrowed, something blue" — to bring the bride luck.

Unlucky signs include: a hunchback or an old woman crossing one's path in the early morning, crossing arms when shaking hands, burning green twigs in the garden, losing one's wedding ring, two spoons in a saucer, rocking an empty cradle, seeing a magpie, spilling salt, crossing one's knife and fork, the ace of spades and the four of clubs, a string of pearls, etc. It is also supposed to be unlucky to meet a funeral procession on one's wedding day, to let one's washing boil over, to give away something pointed, to have a parson on board ship, to open an umbrella in the house and so on.

There is the wide-spread belief that certain signs herald particular events. For example: an itching nose means something new, a cat washing over its ears means a visitor, a dog eating grass is a sign of rain, the ace and queen of spades signify death, a knife sticking in the floor means disaster, a ringing in the ears means either bad news or someone is talking about one, and so we could go on.

Bird calls also have certain meanings attached to them. Hence the barn owl's cry means death, the cuckoo's call means a wish fulfilled, the green woodpecker's cry is a sign of rain, etc. Also a raven on the roof heralds bad luck, killing a plover means losing a lover, and as we have said, seeing a magpie implies coming sorrow.

It is also unlucky to recount a dream before breakfast; and dreams themselves have many interpretations attached to them. To dream of a flood heralds misfortune; to dream of chickens, fish, children or rain, means good luck; to dream of owls means an accident is coming; to dream of breaking ice means one will soon be moving etc. Amongst the flood of occult literature there are many so-called Egyptian dream books which go into the interpretation of all kinds of dreams.

Yet above all the din of the soothsayers we hear the clear words of the Scriptures, "If a prophet arises among you, or a dreamer of dreams, and gives you a sign or a wonder ... you shall not listen to the words of that prophet or to that dreamer of dreams" (Deut. 13:1—3), and, "An evil and an adulterous generation seeks after a sign" (Matt. 12:39). Jesus Himself warned the people of His day with the words, "You hypocrites. You know how to interpret the appearance of earth and sky; but why do you not know how to interpret the present time?" (Lk. 12:56). The same question is valid today.

Palmistry. For a consideration of the subject of palmistry one can turn to the chapter on fortune-telling in

my book *Between Christ and Satan*. So as not to duplicate
what has already been written there, I will only quote one
example here to demonstrate the effects of palmistry.

107. A man practised palmistry for many years. He also
had the ability to heal people through mesmerism. There
came a time when he wanted to become a Christian but he
discovered within himself a strong inner resistance to this
idea. Each time he came into contact with Christian things
this resistance would develope into a strong pressure and
inner conflict.

Psycho-analysis. The next subject on our list
to discuss is psycho-analysis, although many doctors and
psychotherapists will be alarmed at the thought of this.
However, I would beg them to reserve their bitterness and
anger till later. Before I start I would like to say that I am
in complete agreement with the use of psychotherapy when
it is practised by believing Christians. But not every psychotherapist who claims to be a Christian is in fact a Christian. It is unfortunate, but in Christendom today the pre-
cepts of the Bible are clouded over. By definition, a real
Christian is someone who by the grace of God has been
converted and born again of the Holy Spirit. If this has
been the psychotherapist's experience then I would be
prepared to support him in his work. And men such as this
do exist.

It would be good if at this point we could quote just one
good example against all the confusion of the occult world.
I do know of a Christian psychotherapist who realises that
she is responsible before God in the work that she does.
She seeks not only to psycho-analyse her patients but also
to lead them to a living faith in Christ. I can personally
testify that many of her patients have been converted
through her work. She is a real channel of blessing to many.

Unfortunately, positive examples of this nature are hard to come by. In over 30 years of counselling people I have found that much of the work of many psychotherapists and psycho-analysts is questionable. A Swiss graduate once said to me jokingly, "Psychotherapists can usually take the watch apart but they can't put it together again." But this to me is not the main issue. Basically, psycho-analysis when practised by a non-Christian doctor is a form of counselling without God. Psycho-analysis, one might say, is the profane counterpart to confession. Yet confession, as the Bible sees it, has more advantages than psycho-analysis. Confession is of one's own free will, whereas psycho-analysis requires hours of delving into the subconscious areas of the mind. Confession brings a person face to face with God. Psycho-analysis often relegates important religious questions to the level of environmental or educational factors. Psycho-analysis in fact seeks to dissect the very centre of man's spiritual life and to just resolve it into a number of complexes. Occasionally the medical profession refers to the dangers of psycho-analysis. One can see this in particular in Dr. Speer's book entitled *Der Arzt als Persönlichkeit*. The most important factor to remember then, is, whether the psycho-analyst is a Christian or not. If he is, then he will have a respect for the religious questions and problems of the patient. I will give a few examples now, drawn from my own counselling experiences, of some almost inexcusable psycho-analytical treatments.

108. A university graduate was treated initially by a specialist in internal diseases, and then later by a psychotherapist. He was actually suffering from some nervous and psychical disturbances. The patient was very disappointed with the psychotherapist's treatment. He told me that the man merely sought to uncover his failings, weaknesses of character and repressions, without taking the question of

guilt seriously. The psychotherapist had carefully analysed the patient's confused dreams, but had ignored his reactions to sin etc. The patient had been finally discharged as incurable. He told me that the doctor had completely disregarded the question of God. In addition to this none of the doctors he had consulted had shown any interest in his involvement in occultism. The truth was that the patient had been an active spiritist for a number of years, indulging in both black and white magic and fortune-telling. His nervous disturbances had only appeared after his having come into contact with occultism. The doctors had therefore failed to consider two very vital factors in the history of the patient's illness. Firstly his sense of guilt before God, and secondly his previous occult history.

109. A 54-year-old woman came to me for counselling. She had been to a psychotherapist for treatment but had subsequently developed symptoms of paralysis and a nervous twiching in her hands. In addition to this the woman's faith had been brought into utter confusion by the treatment. I had the impression that the therapy had been incomplete for it should have been possible to get rid of the newly appeared paralysis.

110. A Christian psychiatrist I know allowed himself to be used as a guinea-pig during his period of training. He was in the process psycho-analysed by the professor of a psychosomatic seminary. He told me about the experience and left me in no doubt concerning his feelings about it. The analysis had been such a source of trouble to him that he had been in danger of losing his own faith. He had had to spend hours in meditation on the Word of God and in prayer in order to prevent his faith from being completely wrecked. Today this psychiatrist is opposed to the use of psycho-analysis by non-Christians. Again, when we use the term 'non-Christian', it is not just a matter of going to

church or not. A Christian is not someone who has merely
been baptised or confirmed or who goes to church either
occasionally or regularly. No, a Christian is someone who,
according to John 3:3-5, has experienced a fundamental
regeneration through the working of God's Spirit. This
alone makes a person a Christian. Although many doctors
would make the claim that they are Christians, their con-
victions and their attitude to life really have little in common with the New Testament scheme of things.

111. A young woman went to the medical superintendent
of a clinic for psychiatric diseases in Germany for treatment. The professional advice given to her was to stop
going to church and reading her Bible for a couple of years.
He told her not to concern herself with religious matters
at all. He was utterly convinced that there was no such
thing as a devil. This same doctor warned people not to go
to a mission I was holding in the same town. He forbade
the nurses to go to the meetings and took my books away
from the patients. In the course of my counselling work I
discovered that he had already occupied himself with occult matters. This would explain his opposition to everything to do with Christianity.

112. A student who was psycho-analysed in the course of
her medical and psychological training ended up in a terrible psychical state. She had no peace for months. She
could not sleep and found herself to be in a state of inner
turmoil. The analyst had told her that she suffered from a
mother-complex, and this caused her to break off all rela-
tionships with her mother. She left home. In the same way
her teacher said that her religious faith was merely a church-
complex; and so she threw this overboard too. When the
psycho-analysis was complete, the young student was convinced that the majority of people are merely governed by
a series of complexes. In the process though, she herself had

become inwardly torn and distressed. I discovered from both her mother and a professor of medicine that she has lacked an inner sense of peace and has been unsettled in her mind for the last two years.

113. A dean of a certain parish in Switzerland asked me to visit a colleague of his who had been admitted to a hospital suffering from a psychical disease. His colleague, a minister, made an open confession of his sins. Later, however, he complained that the psychotherapist who had treated him had not taken his feelings of guilt seriously, but had merely maintained that they were a by-product of his Christian upbringing. He had said there was no such thing as guilt. I was later able to have a talk with the psychotherapist in question and was able to confirm what the minister had said about him. The doctor only accepted the immanent and intrinsic facts regarding man and the universe. The idea of believing in God, and the idea of guilt and so on, were fictitious. It was pure religious fantasy. And this psychotherapist was supposed to help the minister! It would not have been help; it would have been spiritual murder. I advised the dean to have his colleague removed from the hospital.

114. A woman came to me for counselling at a health resort in Germany. She came in spite of the fact that the psychotherapist who was treating her had warned her not to come. The woman had been coming to the meetings I had been holding and she made an open confession of her sins. I asked her if she had also made a confession before the psychotherapist. She replied that she had not, and added that it would have been impossible for her to have done so. She had so far visited the man on about 40 occasions at a fee of almost £ 2 a session. Yet now within the space of half an hour she had found forgiveness through Christ, and it had cost her nothing. Doctors who are not genuine Chris-

tians should leave psycho-analysis alone. They will only succeed in making a dangerous spiritual mess of things. I repeat again, in the New Testament the term 'disciple' and 'Christian' does not refer to a person who has merely been baptised or who goes to church occasionally. Neither is a disciple of Christ one whose father is a minister or an evangelist, or whose grandmother was a religious person. No, "One must be born again", for without this no one can be a Christian.

Psychography. A psychograph or a planchette is an apparatus used in spiritistic circles as an instrument for receiving written messages from the spirits of the dead. But as Isaiah wrote, "Should not a people consult their God? Should they consult the dead on behalf of the living?" (Is. 8:19).

Since the publication of the third edition of this book a psychic epidemic involving the planchette — or the so-called ouija board — has started. A magazine reported that in 1967 in America about four million ouija boards were sold. A ouija board is a circular board with the letters of the alphabet around the circumference and the numbers from 0 to 9 forming a circle at the centre. The board is used in conjunction with a pendulum or a glass in order to get information through contact with the dead. And thereby those who use it come into bondage. Has the Lord forgotten to help? Is that why the people have to consult demons? No, and sad to say, this is not just a game with the subconscious as some would try to tell us. A glance at the effects will soon show that this is not the case.

Psychometry. Psychometry is another form of fortune-telling and it has been dealt with in more detail in the book *Between Christ and Satan*. Basically psychometry consists of a person who, holding some article in his hands, makes statements about the owner of the article. Some examples:

115. The well-known Dutch clairvoyant, Croiset, lectured on experimental clairvoyance at Kaiserslautern, Germany, in the presence of Professor Bender from Freiburg and Professor Tenhaeff from Utrecht. He asked the audience to give some articles to him. Croiset then stated things about the articles and people concerned which the owners were able to verify as being true.

116. A minister told me the following. During the war his father had been missing for three years. The family did not know whether he was dead or alive. One day a student visited them. He heard that their father was missing and so asked them to give him something which had belonged to the father. They gave him the last postcard they had received. The student concentrated on the card and then said, "He's still alive. He's a prisoner of war somewhere in Northern Siberia." He then went so far as to point out the place on a map of Russia. Only later after the father had returned did the family discover that he had in fact been kept prisoner at the exact spot where the student had indicated.

Rod and Pendulum. In recent years the use of a rod and pendulum has been elevated to the level of a science called radiesthesia. It is therefore not quite so easy to assess as other branches of fortune-telling as it has become linked with various hypotheses and presuppositions. However, because the so-called scientific basis of dowsing has been dealt with in the two books *Christian Counselling and Occultism* and *Between Christ and Satan,* I will confine myself here to quoting a few examples.

117. One of my minister friends told me the following story. He said, "I was holding meetings at a place near

Zurich. I found that people flocked to see me in the time
set aside for counselling. To my surprise over half of those
who came wanted to speak about things relating to occultism. One of the people who came to be counselled was a
man who had practised using a pendulum and who had
other remarkable gifts. He used a book by an Abbé Mermet
for reference, but he also had a lot of personal experience
to draw on. With the aid of the pendulum he was able to
diagnose diseases, to determine the herbal medicine necessary for treatment, and even to locate the bodies of people
who had been drowned in Lake Zurich. He could also
supply one with other information about dead or missing
people. As he talked with me I found I could not answer
his exact scientific arguments. I was just not qualified
enough to argue with him on the matter. It all seemed so
plausible. Then God put a question in my mind to ask him.
It shed light on the whole problem. I asked him if he had
ever suffered anything as a result of these gifts. It was then
that he told me of an occasion when he had once used his
pendulum to look for a gold bracelet lost in the mountains.
He had slipped and begun to fall and slide down the mountain side. Only at the last moment was he able to get a
foothold. The next night he had been awakened by a dark
figure who had physically fought with him. As he was
being overpowered in his terror he had called out the name
'Jesus'. The figure had disappeared immediately."

118. A Christian worker from Zurich shared the following
experience with me. A 50-year-old woman had been ill for
a long time. A family she knew advised her to seek the
help of a pendulum practitioner. The man in question had
some different brands of tea and he used a pendulum to
single one of them out for the woman to take home. It
never occured to her that she was involving herself with
sorcery, but later when she heard a talk on the subject she

was worried and came to the minister for advice. She was quite sure that she had suffered no ill-effects from what she had done. Anyway the minister, the man who was telling me the story, was concerned for her and so prayed with her. A few months later the woman reappeared. She told him about what had taken place since their first meeting. It was as if scales had fallen from her eyes, she said, and she had realised that she really had been under a ban of sorcery. However, since the counselling session she had been delivered from it, for it was only after that time that she had seen how really burdened she had previously been. But now the fog around her had gone. Her Christian life had been entirely changed.

119. An expectant mother allowed a pendulum practitioner to use a pendulum over her unborn child to determine whether it was a boy or girl. Both of the woman's children were treated in this way and today they are both oppressed and burdened as a result of it.

120. A pipe burst in a salt mine. A pendulum practitioner was fetched in to find out where the burst had occurred. The man asked for a plan of the buildings. He then took a pendulum and by means of the plan determined where the burst had occurred. After a search he was proved to be correct. The man later said, "You could have spared me the journey and merely sent the plan to me by itself."

121. A clergyman from Switzerland practised using a pendulum for several years. His colleagues often warned him about the dangers involved. One day he fell in front of a train and lost his legs. They were both amputated but afterwards the wounds refused to heal. Sometime after this some large holes broke open around the wounds and hundreds of large maggots came out of the holes. He died in this state.

122. A 56-year-old woman had often had a pendulum used over her as a child and had also repeatedly been to fortune-tellers. For years now, she has suffered from depressions and a vicious temper.

123. A pendulum was used over a young man to combat an illness. After the treatment he felt a certain amount of relief but at the same time he developed a compulsion neurosis causing him to swear and blaspheme. It was because of this that he had sought counselling help. He committed his life to Christ and the neurosis disappeared.

The use of a rod or pendulum either in the physical or mental form is basically mediumistic — even in the cases where it appears to be quite harmless, or when it is allegedly based on scientific principles, or when it hides behind a Christian facade. If it had been possible to prove that the use of a pendulum was scientifically demonstrable, it would have been done so long ago because the pendulum has been known and used for thousands of years. We could not pretend that the present state of our scientific knowledge is so primitive. Counselling work reveals the damage which is typical of all mediumistic and magical practices. For this reason this strange science of 'radiesthesia' is on the same level as other occult arts. "By their fruits you shall know them" (Matt 7:20).

Screening. In some areas of Europe the idea of screening or shielding one's house and out-buildings is spreading like a plague. Dowsers and pendulum practitioners state that there are rays connected with the earth that are damaging to the health. However, they add that these rays can be screened off by means of certain small boxes. I have personally opened up some of these boxes and they usually contain a small piece of copper wire or copper plate. They cost about two to three shillings to make but are sold for anything up to ten pounds. It is rather obvious what we are up against here. The existence of these so-called earth rays has never been proved. They are unrelated to both the gravitational and electrical fields of the earth as well as to the earth's radioactivity. Already in the 19th century Helmholtz denied their existence. Today, well-known geologists and physicists, as for example Professor Pump, Professor Kirchenheimer and Professor Paskual Jordan of Germany, also deny that they exist. But two possibilities remain. Some animals and some people are sensitive to the earth's magnetic field. But if this were the case here, then one should rather rely on scientific instruments to measure the effects rather than on a small box, or a rod or pendulum. The second possibility is to assume that the world has a mediumistic field which can be clairvoyantly perceived through the mediumistic powers of dowsers and pendulum practitioners and the like. This assumption, although not altogether groundless, has yet to be proved and remains clothed in a mystical aura of darkness. Whatever the case, though, a reliance upon a shielding apparatus and upon radiesthesia is not without its dangers. If man is threatened in this way why does he not turn to God for His protection? "He who dwells in the shelter of the Most High, who abides in the shadow of the Almighty, will say to the Lord, 'My refuge and my fortress; my God in whom I trust'" (Psalm 91).

Significant Dates and Days. The next topic to discuss in our varied list of superstitious customs is the special significance of certain dates and days. It is really humiliating how man, who God ordained to rule the earth, has subjected himself so slavishly to the world. First some examples.

124. In the Weser valley in Germany April 1st is considered to be an unlucky day, so no one, not even an apprentice, would begin a new job on that day.

125. A minister told me about the following custom in his parish. On Christmas eve when the church bells are rung the farmers tie straw round their fruit trees, repeating the names of the Trinity and a magical spell at the same time. The bell ringer is tipped to ring the bells longer than usual so that the farmers can tie the straw around as many trees as possible. On such occasions one finds the whole family in the orchard. The minister has spoken against the custom each Christmas, but the practice continues.

126. In Würzburg, Germany, I heard that many people wash their purses out on New Year's eve in one of the fountains of the town. This is to ensure that they don't run out of money during the coming year.

Habits and ideas and customs like this exist everywhere. Some people for example place eggs under their hens on Good Friday in order to get more chicks. Others say that if a girl wants to get married she is to cut a twig from a tree on the 4th of December, and she will have a bridegroom before it blossoms. At Christmas time people shake the trees for good luck. To eat an apple on New Year's day or on Whit Sunday will make one healthy. Another custom is to fetch water from a stream on the night before Easter Day and to sprinkle it on the sick. April 1st is an unlucky day. May 1st is a lucky day. Children born on a Sunday will be lucky, and May-children should also meet with good fortune. Friday-children are supposed to be unlucky. Many farming laws are also based on such customs, and people predict the weather in the same way. For example if it rains on St. Swithin's day it means it will rain for the next 40 days. Fog too early in April means floods in June, and so we could go on. Yet the words of the apostle remain unaltered, "You observe days, and months, and seasons, and years! I am afraid I have laboured over you in vain" (Gal. 4:10—11).

S p i r i t i s m . Today spiritism has developed into a world-wide movement. Professor Blanke of Zurich estimated that at present it numbers about 70 million adherents drawn from all kinds of religious backgrounds. The subject is treated in some detail in the book *Between Christ and Satan* and so we will not repeat ourselves here. Ways in which one can encounter spiritism include spiritistic visions, table-lifting, glass-moving, automatic writing, speaking in trance, materializations (alleged appearances of the dead), excursion of the soul (the wandering of the souls of the living), telekinesis (the moving of objects with no physical means), levitation (lifting of people and objects — an imitation of the ascension), apports (the appearance and disappearance of objects in closed rooms etc.), and also magic defence and magic persecution which also exist in the spiritistical realm. The appearance of apparitions and ghosts, too, can be included in the list. And last but not least, we have spiritualism and other similar spiritistic religious cults. To glimpse something of the problems posed by these demonic proceedings we will look at some examples.

127. A 65-year-old woman lived in a house where spiritistic meetings were held. At night between 12 and 1 o'clock a terrific noise would start up in the house. The furniture would move and objects would be thrown through the air. On one particular night 40 glasses of bottled fruit and vegetables were smashed in the cellar, although they had been in a locked room. In the end the woman moved. She found herself no longer haunted but each night at the same time she felt as if she was being gripped about the throat and

choked. Whenever she called on the name of Jesus the attacks immediately stopped.

128. A Christian social worker was at a holiday home. At night she heard sounds of knocking. When because of her fear she started to pray, she was choked. She inquired about the house's previous owners and discovered that some members of the S.S. had held spiritistic meetings in her room during the war. The woman asked the advice of a Christian man. The man prayed that the poltergeist would leave the room. His wife suddenly started to suffer from depression. This lasted for about ten weeks.

129. A woman told me that a neighbour of hers was a spiritist with the gift of clairvoyance. The spiritist had once appeared at her door and said, "Your child is in great danger. Please be careful." Two weeks later the child was run over and killed by a car. The spiritist also died in a terrible way.

130. A Christian woman once visited a spiritist to receive magical treatment. Immediately after this she lost her assurance of salvation. She began to be depressed and to have suicidal thoughts, and in addition to this lost all restraint towards alcohol, cigarettes and in her sex life.

131. A woman went to some spiritistic meetings for a number of years. In the end she was able herself to contact the spirits without the aid of the medium. She was able to see and talk to these spirits during the day as if they were her relatives. Her children are prone to depressions and suffer from suicidal thoughts.

132. A spiritist told me that he had had a guide from the other side for 30 years. This guide told him what to do and he always obeyed. He was once ordered to find and visit a married couple who had also made contact with the other side. Till then, though, they had not learnt fully

how to communicate with the spirit world. This spirit from the other side gave the spiritist the exact address of the young married couple. The address was correct. The couple told the spiritist that they had begun to practise table-lifting but had not completely mastered the technique. The spiritist therefore taught them how to communicate with the spirits. He was also told by his guide that he would have an important part to play in eternity when he died. Because he had been so loyal to spiritsm over the years he would be given a high position with the spirits of the next world. The spiritist believed implicitly in what he had been told and what he had been promised. At the end of our conversation he said, "One day you will recognise me in eternity." When I pointed out to him the danger of communicating with spirits in this way, he merely replied, "Oh, you're just blind."

133. An 11-year-old boy used to be a terrible bed-wetter. His parents tried everything to cure him, but both they and the doctor failed. In the end the mother went to a spiritist who practised black magic. Some clothing of the child was magically stroked. The boy had to wear the piece of clothing and from then on he was cured of his bed-wetting. Later, when he was a young man, he tried to commit suicide. It happened that one night his sister, who was a Christian, was very troubled and so began to pray for her brother. All at once she was terrified as she heard him cry out. Her brother rushed into her room from his own bedroom and confessed to her that he had tried to commit suicide. He said that he had suddenly seen her face in front of himself as he was putting the noose around his neck. It is a fact that experimenting with magic and spiritism often leads to depressions and suicidal thoughts.

A special mention must be made in this section of Brasilian spiritism. Brasil is a spiritistic stronghold. One can find almost all forms of spiritism there, ranging from the socially orientated Kardec spiritism to the criminal forms in the Macumba cult.

One cannot but praise in a certain way the charitable work of groups belonging to the Kardec movement. They have built schools, hospitals, childrens' homes, lodging houses, conference halls and many similar places. In Curitiba I visited the *Albergo noturno*. The woman in charge, a charming person, willingly gave us all the information we needed, and told us proudly, "We have already 30 million members in Brasil alone. Within 20 years this should have risen to maybe half the population." It is a fact, spiritism is growing continually.

I was interested to hear of the motive behind their work. The woman I have just mentioned explained, "People are reincarnated after considerable intervals of time. Depending on whether we have done good or evil in this life we either ascend or descend in the next life." They share this belief with many of the religions of the East. Basically it is the way of salvation by works. Yet it has nothing in common with what the Bible teaches.

A consideration of the criminal forms of spiritism in Brasil will be left till the section dealing with the Umbanda and the Macumba cults.

Finally, this section would not be complete without a mention of the religious form of spiritism which is found in Great Britain and America in particular. In visiting Britain I have seen that there are many, many spiritualist churches spread throughout the country. In their services the sermon is not preached by a minister but instead by a medium speaking under the influence of spirits from the other side. The person speaks in a trance and thereby obtains revelations from the departed. Yet instead of a long discussion on the matter, suffice it to say that the Scriptures point out quite simply that such practices are an abomination to God. One can find this written in Lev. 20:27 and Deut. 18:10-12.

Superstition. Superstition itself, although a religious kind of attitude, is an attitude divorced from God. It carries with it some of the most nonsensical decisions and actions. We can best illustrate this by reference to an example taken from Johann Kruse's book, *Witches Among Us.*

134. Three weeks after her wedding a woman was admitted to a hospital in Halten, Germany. She was suffering from some terrible injuries from which she later died. However, before this happened she was able to tell the hospital staff that her injuries were the result of beatings she had received at the hands of her husband and his family. A fortune-teller from Gelsenkirchen had said that she was a witch. It had so happened that just after she had married, an epidemic had broken out among the cattle on her parents-in-law's farm. It was because of this that they had called in the fortune-teller. On the fortune-teller's advice the unfortunate young woman had been locked up in a darkened room and slowly tortured to death through continual beatings and starvation. The family, convinced of all that the fortune-teller had said, carried her orders out to the letter. Later they were all arrested, together with the fortune-teller.

135. I heard the following story from a minister. A man had once come and asked him if he could have his child baptised the following Sunday. However, when he discovered that there were two baptisms arranged already for that Sunday the man asked to have his child's baptism postponed to a later date because he believed it to be un-

lucky to have three children baptised on the same day. Unable to convince the man otherwise, the minister agreed.

There are many superstitious ideas, especially regarding weddings and baptisms. People say that the first place a mother must go to after childbirth is to the church, and she must not talk to anyone on the way. It is also supposed to be unlucky to take a baby out in its pram before the baptism. Catching the bouquet at a wedding is supposed to bring luck. Carrying the bride across the threshold is also considered lucky, and so we could go on. But if we were to "trust in the Lord with all our hearts, and in all our ways to acknowledge him," there would be no room in our lives for these superstitious customs and ideas.

Telepathy. One could easily form the impression on reading this book that all mediumistic powers are evil. However, in my own mind this is not quite the case. There does seem to exist a small band of neutral mediumism. This can be best seen in the phenomenon of telepathy.

One neutral form of telepathy exists between two people who love each other. The stronger the love the greater the harmony and link between their souls. Such people often feel or think the same things without actually speaking to one another. This is the telepathy of love, and it is the best form of all telepathy.

I have also found a neutral form of telepathy among most primitive tribes people with whom I have had contact. However, the word primitive is not quite the right word, since these tribes have often got greater and more developed powers of mind than we civilised people. One of my friends who is a young Lap from Scandinavia had a chief who possessed telepathic powers. These powers allowed the chief to contact or call the various members of his tribe. The amazing thing was that by varying the call each member of the tribe knew when he personally was being contacted or summoned. But then the chief became a Christian. I asked him later, "Did you lose your telepathic powers when you became a Christian?" "Only partially", was his reply. "I can now only contact members of my family to tell them things, but I can't contact the rest of the tribe now or summon anyone." This was very interesting to hear first-hand. I therefore went on to ask him, "Do you think that these telepathic powers are mediumistic or demonic?" "They can't be demonic", he replied, "because I can be praying at the same time as I receive a call from my mother or my brothers. But I feel there is something demonic about being able to summon people because when I became a Christian I lost this particular ability to control my tribe. In the family, though, I think that as a means of contact between those who mutually love one another it can't be demonic."

I was surprised to hear what he had to say in that he too drew a line between neutral and demonic forms of telepathy.

Yet it must be repeated that neutral powers of telepathy comprise only a small part of all telepathic powers. And there is also no real proof that the ability of this Scandinavian chief was in fact only a neutral gift rather than some mediumistic effect resulting from his former demonic powers.

We must be very careful when dealing with these things for the devil is for ever trying to seduce believers. I have found in my counselling work many occult forms of telepathy in the field of spiritistic practices as well as in the realm of clairvoyance. Occult telepathy is as dangerous as any other form of occult activity. But to deny that powers of telepathy actually exist is a sign of intellectual stupidity.

Tongues Movements. A heading 'tongues movements' will at once conjure up two questions in people's minds. Anyone familiar with the phenomenon of speaking in tongues will immediately ask, "How can the author write about a subject like this in a book called *The Devil's Alphabet?*" This can soon be answered. This section deals only with imitation forms of tongues speaking, not with the genuine gift of the Holy Spirit mentioned in 1 Cor. 12:10.

The second question will arise in the minds of those outside the Christian sphere. They will be asking, "What is a tongues movement?" This question can also be answered quite briefly by way of introduction. One can find all over the world today both churches and people who speak or sing in unknown languages in a state of ecstacy. This phenomenon is called 'speaking in tongues' and people attempt to link it with certain passages in the Bible.

Why do we have to discuss the new tongues movements in a book on superstition? It is not out of malice or a bad critical spirit that we do so. No, our aim is to protect the Body of Christ against an influx of extremism and demonic powers.

Is the warning necessary? Indeed yes. There has already been one outbreak of tongues speaking this century. At the turn of the century a tongues movement burst into life in the spiritistic stronghold of Los Angeles. The resultant bad effects of this movement are quite well-known. Much has been written about it since then.

In 1960 another tongues movement had its beginning in Los Angeles, and it has since taken root all over the world, stirring up much unrest in the Church of Christ. The turmoil in the United States was so great for example, that the government set up a commission consisting of a psychiatrist, a Lutheran minister and a psychologist to investigate the disturbing phenomenon.

Let us have a quick look at the roots of the problem as we find it in the New Testament. The phenomenon of tongues speaking is mentioned in the following passages: Mk. 16:17; Acts 2:4, 10:46, 19:6; 1 Cor. 12-14.

At the very outset let me assure people that I believe most strongly in these passages and in the Holy Spirit's gift of speaking in tongues. I do not wish to take away anything from the Scriptures.

But the question which now arises is whether or not today's tongues movements are in any way related to the spiritual gifts of the New Testament. Many if not most men of God would say they are not. Why? Well first of all there have been various epochs of revelation in the history of salvation. The exodus of the Israelites from Egypt and the time of the plagues represents one epoch. The gifts of quails and manna in the wilderness heralded a second epoch ending with the entry of Israel into the promised land. And so it has gone on through history to the present day. The spiritual gift of tongues had its time up till the forming of the canon of the New Testament.

When the canons were fixed at Jamnia and Joppa that particular epoch of revelation ended. Today we live in the era of the Word of God. The Holy Spirit reveals Himself in His Word, in His Church and also in the guidance of each individual child of God. So we find that most mature Christians distance themselves from today's tongues movements, especially as they observe the way in which it develops.

In my travels through more than 100 different countries I have witnessed some strange forms of tongues-speaking. I can best quote a couple of examples to illustrate what I mean.

136. In San Diego, California, a woman came to be counselled. She told me that she had visited the meetings of a

certain Pentecostal brother. This preacher had told the audience, "Only those who have spoken in tongues have been baptised in the Holy Spirit." He then said that if anyone was interested in receiving the Holy Spirit they should stay behind after the main meeting. The woman had done so. When the Pentecostal minister laid hands on her she fell to the ground unconscious. When she awoke she was filled with a terrible fear. Some of the people around her said, however, "You've spoken in tongues wonderfully." But she had had enough of this 'baptism of the Spirit'. Because of this experience she lost her assurance of salvation and her peace with God. This is the reason she had come for counselling. By God's grace her faith was restored, but she never intends to visit another 'Pentecostal mission'.

If a person loses his assurance through this much praised 'baptism of the Spirit' it means that the experience is really from the pit rather than from the Holy Spirit. Moreover, when Pentecostals assert that speaking in tongues is the sole proof of the baptism of the Holy Spirit they slip into heresy. It is just not true. The gift of tongues mentioned by Paul in 1 Cor. 12 is one of the least of the gifts and not the greatest!

137. I have twice spoken at missionary conferences in Japan. Once at the large conference in Karuizawa an American minister caused quite a stir. The night before the conference he arrived and said that the Holy Spirit had told him to go and speak there. However, the conference's president said, "If that were true then the Holy Spirit would have told me as well." After quite a struggle the minister and some other 'Pentecostal brothers' arranged some parallel meetings. A few inquisitive missionaries visited one of these meetings but they learnt such a lesson that they did not want to go again. This strange man stood up and

prayed and sang and preached in tongues without any interpretation. No one there really knew what was going on. Afterwards one of the missionaries asked the minister, "How are you supposed to get this gift of tongues?" The minister replied, "If you repeat a short prayer like 'Lord help me' five or six hundred times then you will suddenly find yourself speaking in tongues." Those were his instructions! And this is called a gift of the Holy Spirit! It has nothing to do with the Holy Spirit; it is merely the training of the subconscious, and is more readily comparable to the automatic speaking and writing one finds in spiritistic circles.

The observations I have made all over the world are so terrifying that people must be warned about these tongues movements. Lack of space prevents us from pursuing the matter further, but if anyone wants to read more on the subject they can read the booklet I have written entitled *The Strife of Tongues*.

Transference. Occult transference introduces us to another mysterious area of sorcery and magic. It occurs also in the spiritual lives of Christians in different forms. In the section on death magic we have already dealt in some way with transferences from living people onto the dead. The first example we will quote is again illustrative of this.

138. A 20-year-old girl died. A woman in the neighbourhood had a large red growth on her throat and she went to the mortuary to get the dead girl to take it with her to the grave. Some magical words were spoken and transference took place. The strange thing is that the growth actually did disappear after this.

People have again and again confessed to me that they have had a kind of psychical shock when they have looked at a corpse or at the body of a person who has committed suicide. Some have said that this has effected them for years afterwards. Two examples of this.

139. A 16-year-old youth saw the body of a person who had just committed suicide being pulled from the water. He was ever after plagued with thoughts of suicide. An inner voice continually used to say to him, "Hang yourself." Because of this he had a nervous breakdown before he was 25.

140. A girl arrived at a river just as the body of an eight-year-old child was being pulled out. She had just been drowned. The girl felt a shock go right through her, and she did not recover from it for 15 years. She was later filled with fear whenever she went near water or even over a bridge.

Both these cases describe a type of transference of a suggestive nature.

In counselling people it has often been told me that occult abilities, as for example being able to dowse or charm, can be transferred from occultists to other people. A Christian should never allow himself to be used as a guinea-pig for occult demonstrations. Again some examples.

141. A Christian worker had a pendulum practitioner on his church council. The elder considered his hobby to be a scientific practice. On one occasion the minister himself tried to divine with a divining rod. Nothing happened. The elder therefore stood behind him and held his forearms. The rod immediately jerked in his hands. Thereafter the minister was able to dowse by himself. However, he at the same time began to have depressions and was troubled in his faith. He prayed a lot with his wife about these psychical disturbances and it became clear to him that the transference of dowsing ability had triggered off the depressions.

He confessed his sin and was thereby delivered from the depressions and his dowsing ability.

142. A minister allowed a dowser to transfer his ability to him. He could afterwards use a divining rod to find water himself.

143. A woman who had practised black magic all her life found it impossible to die. Like many magic charmers she first had to transfer her magical healing powers on to someone else before she was able to die. As she had no relatives she passed her abilities on to one of the neighbours. When the neighbour, too, was near to death she found herself in the same position. She could only die peacefully when one of her granddaughters had taken over the powers of healing. The granddaughter at once began to suffer from severe cramp, and this lasted for eight months. The doctors were unable to diagnose what was wrong. However, in the end the cramp disappeared.

144. I know of a man who had the power to use mesmerism and who passed his ability on to his eldest son before he died.

In the field of love magic quite a lot of transference is involved. We must say again, that the experiences we are dealing with are not those of the mentally ill who are suffering from sexual hallucinations, but rather those of healthy people. There is a clear difference, because those who are occultly plagued can defend themselves through prayer. In addition to this the oppression involved disappears with distance. A schizophrenic suffering from sexual hallucinations and who attributes this to some other person continues to experience the hallucination even when the person is thousands of miles away. An example will make this clear.

145. A girl who had lived a morally good life went to some evening classes. Her teacher was an active spiritist.

The girl was very good looking. During the lessons she felt that the teacher was somehow making approaches towards her. She started experiencing things she had never experienced before. She felt sometimes as if she was having sexual intercourse with him at a distance. At the same time she started to have prophetic dreams and telepathic experiences. When she went on holiday the strange relationship continued but she noticed that the teacher's influence decreased the further she was away. The magical sexual intercourse never took place at distances greater than ten miles.

146. One counselling experience brought a fact to light that I had already met on a number of previous occasions. A powerful spiritistic medium had an accident. The woman fractured both her knee and her pelvis. She was in plaster for three months. However, in the third month she had a miscarriage. The doctor was very surprised because according to the state of the embryo she had only been two months pregnant. He questioned the woman and asked her if she had had any relationship with a man. But he really knew that this was impossible because the lower half of the woman had been in plaster. The plastercast was now removed and a fresh one put on for a further period of three months. Again in the third month the woman had another miscarriage. It was then she admitted that she was a medium and that she had been having psychical sexual intercourse with her husband which had enabled her to conceive.

It is difficult to accept this last example as fact if we rely on our human understanding. Teleplasmic processes like this take place in spiritism more than anywhere else. Hence spiritistic apports also exist in the realm of sexual love, but it is here that the phenomena become the most repulsive. I have many instances of this in my files, but I would not dare publish all this ghastly material. Missionaries tell us of similar occurrences on the mission fields. As an inner protection it is best that we subject our minds and thoughts to the discipline of the Holy Spirit, submitting them to the sprinkling of the shed blood of Christ.

Transferences can also occur in connection with an intensive prayer life. Anyone praying earnestly for an oppressed person must unreservedly place himself under Christ's protection. Otherwise there is a risk of transference. This applies particularly in connection with occult subjection, demonization and possession. A few examples of this.

147. A woman prayed for a person who had attempted to commit suicide. In doing so she started to have similar thoughts.

148. A Christian prayed for another man who was psychically ill and who suffered from suicidal thoughts. In the end this Christian minister started having similar thoughts. The man who had been ill later shot himself. The minister on the same day also had to battle against strong thoughts of suicide although he did not know that the other man he was praying for had killed himself.

149. A Pentecostal minister on many occasions laid hands on a man who was ill. He later developed the same illness himself. He died from the illness.

150. A Salvation Army officer prayed for a man who had subscribed himself to the devil. The man was also a sadist. After some months of intensive prayer the officer began to take pleasure in beating his own wife and one night of the full moon he told her, "I would like to get in contact with the underworld tonight."

151. For a long time a nurse helped in counselling a prostitute. She started praying earnestly for the girl. The prostitute was entirely liberated from her past way of life. The

nurse, however, was afterwards dreadfully plagued with
temptations of this nature. She started to suffer from an
unrestrained sexual craving which she had never known
before. Through her intersession a transference had occurred. Deliverance on the one side had been countered by an
oppression on the other.

152. A minister who dealt a lot with psychically ill people
was in the habit of letting these people stay with him in
the course of their treatment. Time and time again he was
able to witness their being cured through prayer. However,
as time went on his own child became depressive. After the
laying on of hands according to James chapter 5 the child
was healed. After this, though, the man decided to have
no more people suffering from depressive illnesses stay with
them in the house.

153. A bishop was an active spiritist for years. His daughter, although a good-looking girl, was enslaved to almost
every vice you could think of. She drank heavily, smoked
heavily and took drugs. Her sex life knew no restraint.
Yet her main aim was directed at seducing Christian workers and ministers. Once at a Christian house party her
intelligent questions and answers brought her to the attention of the minister leading it. After talking with her he took
her back to the manse to counsel her further. She said that
although she wanted to become a Christian she was not
able to. The minister tried praying with her, but the girl
just could not pray herself. About to repeat a verse of the
Bible by way of comfort, the minister put his hand on her
shoulder. Immediately he did this he felt a shock go right
through himself. Everything went black and he felt himself
sinking into a bottomless pit. A cry of terror escaped from
his lips. On hearing this some other helpers at the conference rushed into the room closely followed by his wife.
After a few minutes, although it seemed like hours to the

minister, he regained consciousness. The girl looked at him,
and with an evil expression on her face asked him, "Do
you know who I am now? I've shot down others already."
The girl later confessed that she had succeeded in seducing a
well-known Christian worker. She had led the man on and
let him talk to her on theological matters, but then she had
succeeded in making him commit adultery with her. She
even gave his name. After his experince with this demonically affected girl the minister who was telling me the story
was depressed for three weeks. The girl herself later committed suicide; but the minister, by God's grace, was cured
of his depressions. It was then that he visited the other man
who the girl had named, in the hope of perhaps being able
to help him. The story turned out to be true and the man
concerned, after his affair with the girl, gave up all his
Christian work.

   Intersession and counselling are basically a battle against
the unseen powers of darkness. Many have already fallen
on this battle field. We ourselves then must constantly be
armed with the weapons of the Holy Spirit. Paul wrote
in his letter to the Ephesians, "Above all taking the shield
of faith, with which you can quench all the flaming darts
of the evil one."

154. I was told of one very distressing case of transference
by the wife of a missionary in China. Her husband had
once visited an active sorceress when she was dying. This
sorceress in her youth had subscribed herself to the devil,
and wore cords around her arms, which were never to be
untied, as a sign of this. The missionary talked now with
her at her bedside about the gospel, and wrestled with her
soul. He told her that Christ could still save her in spite of
a life spent in the service of the devil. "Try to take this
step", he said. "Undo those cords as a sign of renunciation."
A terrific battle commenced between the gospel and the

evil powers of sorcery. In the end it was the grace of God
that won. In the face of death the woman gave her life to
the Lord. She took a pair of scissors and cut through the
cords. Meanwhile a tragic event took place back at the
missionary's house. His eldest daughter had given her two-
year-old brother a piece of roasted soya-bean. The child
sucked it. Suddenly the soya-bean lodged in his windpipe
and he began to choke. His father could have made an
incision in the windpipe but he was at the bedside of the
sorceress. The mother dare not do this. So the family prayed
over the unconscious son. Suddenly while they were
praying the child opened his eyes and smiled happily at
them all. He then sank back and was dead. The missionary,
his father, returned home soon after this. They discovered
that the child had choked at the same time as the chords
were being cut. Coincidence? Well, a person who knows
nothing of the efficacy of sorcery will say that it was. However, the counselling work of well-known Christian workers suggests the opposite. Transferences exist in which
oppressed people are delivered and others are bound. But
it need not have happened. In the example just mentioned
it could have been avoided if the missionary had consciously placed his whole family under the protection of Jesus
at the time of his dealing with the sorceress. And indeed
special mention should be made of the fact that in cases
where one is dealing with well-known sorcerers and mediums it is extremely advisable to have the help of other
Christians. Two are better than one in such cases, and sometimes a prayer group to back one up is also advisable.
The missionary's wife definitely connected the choking
with her husband's counselling work. But the child's death
was not in vain, for afterwards there was a softening in
the attitude of the church in which they were working.

Nominal Christians and traditional Christians who are

strangers to spiritual warfare will not trust the account of
an example like this. Doctors who are only scientifically
orientated will also no doubt cry out in unbelief. But what
does that matter? The facts of the New Testament which
include the driving of the devils into the 2000 swine entirely bypass the short-sightedness of man.

Umbanda and Macumba. I was introduced to
the Umbanda cult in Porto Alegre by Professor Krebs during a lecture tour of Brasil.

The Umbanda cult which is almost a state religion in
Brasil, is of a composite nature. One can trace its origins
back to the African negro cults brought in by the slaves.
To these were added some Indian magic of the Americas,
some spiritistic elements and some Catholic components.

The Umbanda hierarchy can be described as follows.
The movement's head consists of the Cult Father *(Pia de
Santo)* or the Cult Mother *(Mae de Santo)*. Subject to this
leadership are the *Filhas de Santo*, the holy sons and daughters of the sect. These are in fact the *Sambas*, or in other
words, the mediums.

The outward form of an Umbanda meeting can be divided into four parts. These are firstly sacrifice, by which
those admitted are sprinkled by the blood of an animal,
then the public meeting in which they work themselves up
into a state of ecstasy through hours of dancing, then a
love feast, and lastly the putting in order of the cult objects.

Anyone desiring to know the real nature of these Umbanda religious services will find it difficult to get a clear
answer. The general opinion is that through the dancing
the cult mother is filled with the spirit of her god. She
then blesses the people present, gives them short admoni-
tions, marries couples present, and lays hands on the sick.

Cult members can also dance themselves into a frenzy and thereby be filled with the spirit of the cult god.

One need not waste words in saying that religious meetings like this have nothing in common with true Christianity, even though a number of Christian symbols appear in them.

Macumba paints an even stranger picture. The Umbanda people strongly object when they are linked together with the Macumba cult. They would always say, "Macumba is basically a low criminal form of spiritism whereas Umbanda is a superior spiritual form."

The word Macumba has no simple definition. Many people say that it is derived from an evil Jongo-dancer named Cumba. The magic he practised was therefore called Macumba. Others will say that the word goes back to the spirit of Kiumba, a demon of disaster.

Macumba is a mixture of black magic and a criminal form of spiritism. The cult is openly orientated about the god of evil and disaster. According to the Bible his real name is Lucifer or Baalzebub. This god is supposed to be supported by a whole hierarchy of demons. These are called the exu. The basic aim of Macumba is to find ways and means of persecuting enemies or of defending oneself from enemies. To accomplish this they lay offerings down at crossroads for the exu, whom they believe often frequent such places in their scurrying to and fro. But all this can best be explained by an example.

155. A man visited a Macumba meeting and asked them if his wife could be killed. The leader of the cult took a rag doll and later at midnight held it up to the waning moon. She then stuck a needle into the doll several times and murmured some curses and magical phrases. Finally the doll was laid at some cross roads together with some

sacrificial offerings. This was to remind the demons to kill the man's wife. But the woman did not die. Instead it was the husband who was killed. The sorcery struck therefore not at the guiltless but at the guilty. God never hands over to anyone the reigns of his government. It is He alone who rules over life and death, not the demons.

We will not be going into Macumba in any more detail here because I have done that already in my book, *Jesus auf allen Kontinenten*.

However, there is one other story I must just mention. In Rio de Janerio I got to know a woman who had been the leader of the Macumba cult for 23 years. At the end of this period she had been wonderfully delivered by a mighty act of God. Today she lives as one of Christ's messengers, having already shown many the way to her Redeemer.

Wart Removal. Methods of wart removal are customs of a very doubtful nature, and are usually either suggestive or magical in character. The examples we will look at first of all are illustrative of the suggestive side of this problem.

156. I got to know a doctor living in a town just south of Hannover who had the following way of successfully removing warts. He would stroke the warts of the patients at the same time murmuring the first few lines of the Odyssey, *"Ennepe Musa andron polytropon hos mala polla epathen..."* etc. Since the patients were unable to understand the meaning of the quotation it worked like a magic spell and the warts would disappear.

157. A skin doctor living in Lothringen whom I know quite well has the following rather puzzling method. He tells his young patients to place their hand on a piece of white

paper. Next he traces round the hand with a pencil. He then asks the patients to take the paper home and to mark the positions of their warts on it. When they come to the surgery the second time he takes the piece of paper and throws it on the fire saying, "Well, now all the warts will be gone within a few days." This method is very successful. However, it does not work with adults.

158. The following is a method that actually does work with adults. The warts are rubbed with bacon and a magic spell is repeated at the same time. The bacon is then placed outside near one of the corners of the house or thrown into an open grave. I will not say what the actual words of the spell are, for I am convinced that if I did a lot of people would try the method.

159. A bishop in northern Germany told me about the following custom found in his diocese. In order to remove warts the men sprinkle themselves with some water used in the washing of a female corpse. Women do the same with the water used in washing a male corpse. While they are doing this they repeat a spell found in the 6th and 7th Book of Moses. The warts do in fact disappear. The bishop added that this treatment tends to produce sexual laxity in those who practise it. This agrees with my own observations. But it only happens in the case of magical wart removal and not with suggestive treatments.

Witchcraft. Witchcraft is not only representative of one of the darkest chapters of the Middle Ages but also of the present day. This can be seen quite clearly by reading Kruse's book *Witches Among Us*. The innocent have suffered terribly through this practice. The following short examples actually come from some court records.

160. In 1934 a woman in Glarus was burnt to death in her house because it was said she was a bewitcher of horses.

161. In 1951 two men from the Lüneburge Heath set light to the house of an alleged witch. The old woman was saved but two of her relatives died in the flames.

162. In 1951 a 19-year-old boy in Brunswick killed his own father because he thought he had been bewitched by him. The youth later hanged himself.

One needs a lot of experience and often even the gift of discernment in order to be able to distinguish between the genuine intrigues of black magic and spurious forms of witchcraft.

Yoga. Yoga is basically a Far Eastern and Indian or Hindu system of philosophy and psychology. In writing this section I have had at my disposal the comprehensive work on Patanjali yoga by Mishra called *The Textbook of Yoga Psychology* (Julian Press, New York). Other information has come to me through an Indian professor, Professor de Roy. However, most of my material stems from my travels through India, Thailand and other parts of East Asia. Last but not least there have been several occasions on which I have had to counsel people who have been injured through yoga exercises. All this has given me a fair amount of insight into the matter.

In the space that we have it is impossible to give a complete description of yoga. Perhaps I might be able to do this in a later work.

First of all, though, here are a few notes from the work of Mishra to help clarify the picture. The word yoga itself has a meaning corresponding to the *unio mystica* of German mysticism, that is, the mystical union with the universal spirit. The difference between yoga and German mysticism is that yoga is atheistic in nature whereas the German mystics were engaged in a search for God. Their similarity lies in the fact that they share the idea of self-realisation. Man must aim at attaining to his eternal self through the practice of many exercises in purification. This eternal self or real self is supposed to be a part of the universal or ultimate reality. As we have said, yoga calls this process self-realisation. We can see already that it will always be impossible to harmonize yoga and Christianity.

To give us an even clearer picture we will list a few concise statements on yoga from the already mentioned book:

Every bodily organ is related to the soul.

Every person has a physical and spiritual nature which strive with one another for pre-eminence. A harmony and union of these two natures is to be achieved through psychological exercises.

Man's eternal self is omnipotent, omnipresent and omniscient.

Man's eternal self is both transcendent and immanent; it is without beginning and without end, having neither birth nor death.

Material things are on a lower level than the mind, the intelligence and the spirit.

Yoga includes all branches of physics and metaphysics. Yoga implies a synthesis of the physical and the metaphysical universes.

Heaven and hell are the products of man's mind.

The system of yoga stands behind magic, mysticism and occultism.

Such statements could be multiplied a hundredfold. They reveal that yoga is totally opposed to what the Bible says. It is therefore dangerous for Christians to become susceptible to yoga as they might to the latest bout of flu.

Most systems of yoga can be divided into four convenient stages, at least for the western mind. The first stage embraces remedial gymnastics, breathing exercises, relaxation exercises, exercises in concentration, contemplation and meditation. It would also include what one sometimes calls auto-genous training. It is commonly said that Christians can unhesitatingly participate in this first stage and some doctors even recommend it in the treatment of their patients.

The second stage involves the control of the subconscious. For example, masters of this second stage can control and govern their visceral nervous systems. I have met some of these people and they can do the most astounding feats. They can, simply through concentration, increase or decrease their blood circulation, and hence, for example, can make the lobe of one ear go red at the same time as making the colour drain from the other lobe. One man could induce the crucifixion marks to appear on the palms of his hands, although this is in no way to be considered as a religious miracle. I saw another yogi stick knives through his arms and cheeks. The wounds did not bleed but merely closed up again as the knives were withdrawn and healed within a few hours.

The third stage of yoga goes on to the controlling of the forces of nature. I have heard of Tibetan yogis who through concentration could release enough energy to melt ice. There are others who can make a fire break out without any physical or material aid. Here it seems to be a question of fire-demons. I have actually had things of this nature confessed to me in counselling sessions. Once in Port Elizabeth, South Africa, one such 'fire-master' came to see me. He wanted to get out of the position he was in but he could not do so in his own strength.

The fourth stage of yoga is concerned with the mastery of magic and the cosmic forces. It involves the practice of all spiritistic and magical phenomena, and it is on this stage more than any of the others that I have been able to gather the most material. One person who really opened my eyes on this subject was a man who had been trained in Tibet for 10 years by a master of magic. This person came to me when I was in Australia in order to be counselled. He was quite open about it and said that this fourth stage of yoga is a matter of pure demonical practices. He wanted to be freed from it all. Masters of yoga who have reached the highest level of developement can produce materializations, levitation, telekinesis, states of trance, the excursion of the soul and many other spiritistic phenomena.

What can we say about yoga from the Christian's point of view? Firstly, although it is not a very happy picture, there is a tendency throughout Christendom for people to adopt and to utilize the philosophy and teachings of yoga. As we have said before, a lot of people are of the opinion that only the later stages of yoga are dangerous for Christians. Is this correct?

One thing the West must never imagine is that it alone has reached the heights of wisdom and knowledge. The Eastern world mocks at us today, for as a result of rationalism we have blinded our eyes to half the truth. The East has experience of things, the existence of which the West, in her unbelievable narrow-mindedness, simply denies. Yet even admitting that the East has a perception of things which is stunted in the West, this does not sanction our experimenting in this mediumistic field. Yoga may indeed be harmless to begin with, but it ends dangerously. Yet even the first stage of Yoga is not without its dangers when for example the exercises involved are linked with short Buddhist prayers. I know of Christians who in taking part in such exercises have been made to repeat in chorus short Indian phrases by their teacher. On inquiry it turned out that they were saying things of the nature: "Buddha is the enlightened one", or, "Buddha is supreme". One wonders what Christians are letting themselves in for when they are prepared to repeat Buddhist prayers of this nature. It would be difficult to maintain that exercises in concentration like these are not dangerous.

In point of fact a young man in South Africa told me that after beginning some yoga exercises he found that he was unable to pray as before, and that he lost his Christian faith. I at once advised him to stop practising the exercises, and he did so. It would be good for us if we would keep in mind the words of the apostle Paul when he said, "Has not God made foolish the wisdom of the world? For since, in the wisdom of God, the world did not know God through wisdom, it pleased God through the folly of what we preach to save those who believe. For the Jews demand signs and Greeks seek wisdom, but we preach Christ crucified ... to those who are called ... Christ, the power of God and the wisdom of God" (1 Cor. 1:21—24). What need have we as Christians of the inner 'edification' of these pagan Eastern systems. Have the Scriptures no more to offer than Buddhism or Hinduism? We insult our Lord when we leave the living source of the Bible for these foreign springs whose poisonous contents either kill or paralyse our spiritual lives. And with that we must end the devil's alphabet.

III. The Deliverance that Exists through Christ

1. Almost every one of the examples quoted so far has illustrated the fact that superstitious and occult customs, no matter what form they take, to a greater or lesser extent produce dangerous results. Much of this can be understood as the outworkings of either suggestion or auto-suggestion, for in many cases the influence penetrates to the subconscious areas of one's mind. Although we may consciously laugh at superstition from its logical standpoint, subconsciously we may be tricked into fulfilling what we consciously ridiculed. This fulfilment compulsion exists in conjunction with superstition. The things we either fear or laugh at have a tendency to come true. And this our psychiatrists, psychotherapists and psychologists all recognise, for these are facts which can still be understood by science.

It is when we enter into the area of the magical and the spiritual, into the transcendental and supernatural events which contradict our reason, that the scientist is unable to follow. There exists a higher natural order in which the simple laws of cause and effect no longer hold true. This order does not submit to scientific analysis; it can only be understood by faith. And this world of faith is not a myth and it is not just a product of the imagination. No, it can be recognised and experienced as much through its demonic nature as through its divine nature. Faith actually entails a realization of higher things. The New Testament calls this realization and conviction *elenchos*. For the believer this realisation and *elenchos* is as valid as a mathematical proof. For example, the resurrection cannot be proved scientifically or mathematically, but can only be understood through faith. But the reality of the resurrection is as much a fact to the believer as two times two is to the mathematician. Within this higher natural order we find that the magical is the demonic counterpart to the spiritual things of the Bible. For the Scriptures the matters of prime importance are deliverance, re-creation, completion and perfection, whereas the magical invariably leads to destruction, annihilation, chaos and darkness.

In spite of the fact that this higher world order fails to submit to the ordinary laws of argument and reason, one can still arrive at a certain understanding of its divine and demonic character. Because of the contact and overlapping of the natural world and the spiritual world a picture can be built up in our minds by the various glimpses and statistical data and corroborating evidence we get from it. But in saying this I am not in any way suggesting that we can thereby open up a way to a form of natural theology.

How then do superstition and occultism fit into the picture. The fact is that the magical character of their effects is not recognised by the natural scientist. As long as they fail to fall within the classical framework of disease and illness they will remain incomprehensible to him. Yet even were it possible to classify their effects, terrible errors in diagnosis would still exist. In the same way in which an evangelist may mistake an endogenous depression or schizophrenia for a case of possession, so too can the psychiatrist mistake a case of demonization, occult subjection or possession for a psychosis. In both events it would be a terrible error of judgment. Neither the psychiatrist nor the theologian is completely infallible when it comes to dealing with the psychically ill. Hence, if we refuse to listen to one another or to recognise the limits of our work we have no right to practise our profession.

In order to see at a glance the most frequent symptoms
and effects of occult subjection, we shall now group them
together under three headings. Most of these effects have
been illustrated in some way or another in the examples
we have already quoted, but we will be supplementing the
lists where we think it is necessary.

(i) In the spiritual realm: no sense for spiritual things;
fanaticism; no peace; living according to the law; indiffer-
ence; spiritual pride; Pharisaism; lack of concentration in
relation to the Bible; self-righteousness; cynicism; hardness
of heart; sheer unbelief; religious madness; doubt; closed to
the Holy Spirit; opposition to religion and so on.

(ii) In the psychical realm: anxiety states; extreme cases
of bed-wetting; depressions; self-will; sexual perversion;
lack of restraint; fits of temper; gossiping; kleptomania;
blasphemous thoughts; lust; neuroses; feelings of revenge;
sleepwalking; suicidal thoughts; quarrelling; addiction;
nightmares; alcoholism; unforgiveness; hallucinations;
compulsive actions etc.

(iii) In the organic realm: abnormal attacks and fits; in-
herited oppressions; chronic scalp or skin diseases; prone-
ness to fall; hysterical cramps; paralysis; frequent miscar-
riages; nervous complaints; deafness; St. Vitus' dance;
twitching etc.

However, one cannot assume that these symptoms always point to an occult cause, although this is frequently
the case. There are times, though, when illnesses and oppressions of this nature have a cause which can be medically
substantiated. The only thing we are trying to establish is
that in many cases where people have become involved in
superstition and sorcery these symptoms appear. Yet it can
be added that even if one can prove that there is some natural cause for the illness, this does not rule out the pos-

sibility of occult subjection playing a part. However, we must say again that if the statement, "Occult subjection leads to nervous and psychical complaints", is reversed to imply, "Nervous and psychical complaints are a sign of occult subjection", then a terrible short circuit has taken place. Depressions and the like can be caused by many other things besides occultism.

2. What then must be our attitude to all these effects and oppressions of superstition and occultism? Must we just resign ourselves to them? Can we stop the flow of this wide and turbid stream? Is there any effective defence? In fact, in answer to these questions, much can be done to prevent the growth and spread of occultism and its effects. One easy method is to adopt the attitude that it is all nonsense. I know of psychologists who have lectured brilliantly to this effect. They have said, "Superstition is pure nonsense resulting from a lack of enlightenment." If my opponent does not exist I need not fight him. But anyone who dismisses the subject in this way overlooks the very kernel of the matter. People would be in a better position to combat superstition and occultism if they did but understand its true nature. Unfortunately our very education encourages the spread of superstitious ideas. Our children are early introduced to the idea of witches and sorcery and similar phenomena, both at home and at school. And this occurs mainly through ignorance, for the terrible effects are largely unknown. There is an urgent task before us to rid the scene of fairy tales, stories of witches and magic, and plays and films based on the same subject matter. The picturesque and teachable material of this nature impresses itself deeply into the young child's mind. Depth psychology reminds us of the effect pictures can have on the mind of the young. And these impressions made on one's subconscious mind are seldom eradicated. They are merely covered over by a

façade of intellectualism and logical thought, and one finds that adult life is still to a large extent governed by the material one absorbed in the process of growing up. Adults therefore, although they may laugh at superstition, are up to their necks in it. What is even more inexcusable is when Sunday School children are issued with pamphlets written by Christians containing witch stories. In this I could mention some names, but I will not, so as not to harm anyone. Anyway I have written to the editors in question. It is encouraging to note that in 1949 the South African government in Durban decided to remove all the worse fairy-tales from the country's school books. And in 1950 the papers contained the story that the Japanese ministry of education had set up a committee to combat superstition. But in these so-called days of enlightenment Europe is still far behind.

3. The only real method of defense against the superstitious and the occult is Christ. This brings us back to where we started. It is only through Christ that we can appreciate the depths of magic and superstition, and it is only through Christ that we can overcome them, for He alone has overcome the prince of this world, and only He can overcome Satan's intrigues. Through His death on the cross, and through the power of His resurrection, Christ leads us in triumph with all the defeated powers of the Evil One following in His train. This we will now illustrate by means of some actual cases of deliverance.

163. A 13-year-old boy complained of tiredness and pains in his back. At first his parents thought this was the result of overwork, because, being poor, the boy had to help them in the fields and in the forest each day. When there was no improvement in his condition and it only got worse, the father sent the boy to see the doctor. Following a thorough

examination the doctor affirmed that he was suffering from tuberculosis of the nerves of the spinal cord. He said that it was too late, that the disease had got too much of a hold on the boy, and that the father should have brought the boy to see him much earlier. In dismay the father asked him what he could do. The doctor, knowing of a magic charmer, said to the father, "Go and see this man. He knows more than I do." In the course of time the father found himself in the consulting room of this notorious sorcerer. He noticed on the walls testimonies to the effect that the man had been successful in checking epidemics and in other cases of healing. The man stood the boy in front of a large mirror. He stared at him intently and then said, "There's something terribly wrong with you, sonny. You should have come a lot earlier. Well, we'll see what we can do." He then made three crosses over the boy's body, stroked his spine three times and murmured some sentence in Latin. The boy was then given some Arnica tincture and told to rub it into his back each day. He was to return in a month's time. The charmer also added, "You must believe in me, if you want to be healed." On leaving, the father noticed that all the patients had been given similar bottles of Arnica tincture. In fact, apart from one exception, this is the only medicament the healer advised. No matter whether the patient was suffering from migraine or a dislocation or some physical injury, they were to rub the tincture into their skin. The exception was in the case of blood poisoning, for which the patient was told to apply some hot porridge made from maize to his body. The medicament was not the most essential part of the healing process; priority was given to the magical stroking performed in the name of the Trinity or in the devil's names. The boy went to see the man on three occasions and was subsequently healed through the magical treatment. He grew up to be a healthy young man. When he got married his wife, who was at least a nominal Christian, tried to get him to read his Bible and go to church. It so happened that through hearing the Word of God he decided to become a Christian. He began immediately to suffer from depressions and suicidal thoughts. He told me in the course of counselling that his life had continued normally since the healing, and it was only when he had begun to pray and to read his Bible that the trouble had started. He added that without knowing it the magical healer had subscribed him to the devil. The depressions increased so much that he actually attempted to commit suicide on three occasions. A doctor, on seeing the dose he had taken to poison himself, said, "This should have been enough to kill ten people." As the weeks went by a group of people got together to pray for the young man. In addition to this the men of the church on several occasions prayed for him under the laying on of hands. The battle continued for months, but in the end Christ overcame the 'strong man'. The evil ban was broken. The young man was delivered from the effects of the magical treatment. Where sin abounds, grace abounds all the more.

164. A woman came to me for counselling. In spite of a confession she was unable reach an assurance of salvation. Since her inability to believe resembled the type of resistance one meets in the case of occultly subjected people I asked her about her past. She told me the following story. Her mother had had all her children charmed whenever they had been ill. The children had had to cross their arms while the mother had repeated a magic spell in the name of the Trinity. I asked about her other brothers and sisters and she said they all suffered from depressions and had sexual troubles. Sometimes they wanted to become Christians and they would pray a great deal about this; at other times they would go the other extreme and reject

Christianity altogether. Her sister once said to her, "I'm under an evil spell." It was then that I was able to show this troubled woman the way to Christ and to explain to her everything relating to the overcoming of the effects of occultism. She went home and after battling all night in prayer, by the grace of God she was liberated. She came and saw me a few days later and in her joy told me how she had been delivered, adding that she had never been so happy in all her life.

165. The malicious power of superstition can also be seen in the experience of a minister who, before the last war, became famous for his article against Rosenberg's book, *Myth of the 20th Century.* In what he preached and what he taught he was violently opposed to all forms of superstitious and occult customs. One day he decided to get some convincing evidence with which to refute fortune-telling. He had a very careful and detailed horoscope cast for himself, and thereby hoped to prove that this superstitous idea was invalid through watching the prophecies remain unfulfilled over the subsequent years. However, it did not turn out as he had expected. As time went on he had the unnerving experience of watching the horoscope begin to be fulfilled. And this continued for all of eight years. In the end he realised that he had placed himself under the ban of superstition. He thus repented and once more placed his life in the hands of Jesus Christ. Only now did the horoscope fail in its fulfillment. His life at once altered from the course predicted by the 'cosmobiogram' or horoscope. Had he previously been the victim of suggestion? Had he subconsciously believed in the horoscope? Had he fallen victim to a fulfillment compulsion? Or had the minister been caught within the claws of a demonic form of astrology? It is impossible to say. But whatever the case, Christ proved Himself to be the great Deliverer. The ever tighten-

ing net of superstition had been broken, a feat impossible
in one's own strength, as the man's previous eight years'
experience had shown.

166. A fine example of Christ's power to deliver is afford-
ed us in the answer to a girl's prayer who is now a Christian social worker. The girl's father is a well-known Christian man equipped by God with many spiritual gifts. He
had once invited another man to his house who was occultly subjected, in order to give him some sustained Christian counselling. The oppressed man had experienced terrible states of fear each night and was severely troubled
by this. He felt as if the devil himself was the source of
his complaints. The origin of the attacks was obvious. In
his youth the man had practised a lot of sorcery and he
was now experiencing the unhealthy and demonic effects
of his folly. A group of people prayed for the oppressed man
and the daughter joined them. One night a remarkable
battle took place. The girl continued to pray by herself for
the man, and in her desperation and entreaty she asked the
Lord to remove the man's burden and to place it on herself and then to free her. Suddenly she felt the presence of
some unearthly forces in her room. The next thing she knew
was that she was being thrown to the floor in the grip of
some terrible claws. She could not move and lay there for
hours. The only thing she could do was to groan, "Lord
help me, Lord help me." What the girl experienced that
night was hell. Next morning when it was quite late she
was able to drag herself out of her bedroom into the living
room. Her mother took one glance at her and then cried
out, "Child, what's happened to you?" The girl was very
pale and horribly disfigured. She could hardly say a word
and was completely exhausted. Slowly she told her mother
about the battle she had had in prayer. Her parents told
her and begged her never to do the same again. An hour

later the man she had prayed for came out of his room. He was happy and relaxed, and joyfully told them that God had freed him during the night. His oppression and attacks never recurred. The Lord had answered the girl's prayer of faith and had delivered the man. The girl herself suffered no ill effects, and she quickly recovered from her ordeal of faith.

> Jesus the prisoner's fetters breaks,
>> And bruises Satan's head;
> Power into strengthless souls He speaks,
>> And life into the dead.

A Christian teacher who used to work together with Johannes Seitz told me of some of his experiences. These stories are such wonderful and excellent testimonies to Christ that to publish them cannot fail to bring glory to God. The accounts can still be verified today by a whole host of Christian workers and are repeated here without exaggeration.

167. My story-teller took up a teaching post in a rich farming area. Since the farmers in their contentment and prosperity saw no need of a Saviour, the new teacher went from house to house giving out Christian literature. As the farmers would not go to church, he brought the church to the farmers. One day in the course of his door-to-door visitation he was confronted by a man who asked him, "Do you believe in the messages of your tracts?" "Yes, of course I do. I wouldn't give them out if I didn't", replied the teacher. "Can you really rely on the things being true? Aren't they just a lot of religious jargon?" the farmer went on. The young Christian disciple replied, "These things

have been written by convinced Christians. You can trust them completely." "Ah, that's what I wanted to know", the farmer said. "You remember the tract last Sunday", he went on. "It was about someone being healed by faith. Can your Jesus heal my wife as well?" "I'm convinced that miracles happen today; otherwise Jesus would not be the same yesterday, today and forever", the teacher answered. "I'll take you at your word", said the farmer. "Come and see my wife with me. She's beyond the help of the doctors." "What's wrong with her?" asked the teacher. "It's a nervous disease or something worse", replied the man. "Can your Jesus heal things like that as well?" "Jesus can heal everything, including the things in which man has failed", returned the teacher.

The farmer thus led the way, not into the house as one might have expected, but into the barn. Taking a ladder he climbed up into the loft. The astonished teacher followed him. "Her room is in the corner over there", the farmer said. They came to a heavily secured door. The farmer unlocked the padlock, removed the wide metal bar across it and pushed the teacher into the room beyond. The repulsive atmosphere of the room hit the young man. The walls were smeared with blood and excrement, the windows were barred, and the only piece of furniture was an unmade bed on the far side of the room. The teacher could not retreat because the farmer now stood in the doorway behind him. An evil force seemed to strike home at him. He at once began to pray the words, "Lord cover me with your blood. Protect me from this power of Satan, and stand with me. I don't know what's wrong here but I know you are able to withstand anything." Then the blanket on the bed moved and a pale and horrible face appeared from behind it. It was a woman and for a moment she stared at the intruder. Then she sprang up from the bed, crouched down and made as if to spring like an animal. The teacher stood his ground but continued praying for the Lord's protection. The woman sprang at him as if to scratch his eyes out. Then when she was a foot away from him her hands dropped and she scurried back to the bed. She prepared to spring again and did so only to return to the bed after she had done so. This repeated itself a number of times. She would spring at him and then circle him like a beast would a captured prey. Yet on each occasion when only a foot away she would spring back to the bed. Her rage increased and she began to blaspheme the name of Christ terribly. It even filled her own husband with horror. She tore at her own clothes and lifted them up for the men to see her naked body. The teacher still prayed. It was obvious to him now that the woman was not mentally ill but demon possessed. But he only knew a little about these things. Here he was being thrust into a circumstance he had never really met before first-hand. He prayed that the Lord would order the woman to go back to her bed and lie down quietly. And she did. However, it only lasted a few minutes and then she was up again and renewed her attacks. The struggle began a second time. In the end the teacher had the courage to cry out in a loud voice, "Jesus has overcome." At once the woman went back to her bed, and this time she stayed there and was quiet. The battle appeared to be over.

The farmer advised his visitor to leave now. He bolted the door. "She's never behaved like that before", he said. "That I've never experienced. Do you still think she can be healed?" The teacher, although still exhausted from the battle, replied, "Yes, Christ can still heal your wife. The doctors won't be able to, but if you hand your own life over to Christ and pray for your wife, she can be healed." "I can't pray", he said. "Then begin today", the teacher told him. "Pray for me. I just can't believe she'll ever be all right again. I've got letters from some psychiatrists saying that she is incurable. Even at the psychiatric clinic she behaved like an animal. She tore at her hair and took her clothes off and ran about naked. She's attacked the attendents, ate her own excrement and she does the same here. How can she be helped?" To this the teacher replied, "Why shouldn't God be able to help someone like this? Your wife isn't ill, she's demon possessed, and a doctor won't be able to make them leave. This can only happen through prayer and fasting." The farmer asked anxiously, "But how does a person get like this?" "Through sorcery or superstitious customs or card-laying or magic healing", explained the teacher. "In the case of your wife I got the impression while praying in the room that it is a case of spiritualism. Maybe table-lifting or contact with the dead or something like that." "It could be", said the farmer. "My wife was in the habit of doing things like that." Hearing this the teacher asked him, "Do you realise that this is a serious sin?" "Yes", he replied. "Good, then I will pray for you both." "But my wife's completely mad. The doctors told me she's incurable, and you say she can be healed. I just can't believe it. I can't imagine your God doing a thing like that." By now the two men were at the gate and the teacher left.

The next Sunday he again went around to the houses giving out his tracts. As he approached the house of the possessed woman he really wanted to hurry right past it. But the farmer saw him and called him over. "I must show you something", he said. The teacher thought, "Now we're off to the loft again." But he was mistaken for the farmer led him into the kitchen. And there, cooking the midday meal was his wife. She did not recognise him, and the teacher himself avoided talking about her illness. However, his heart was flooded with thankfullness to the Lord who had revealed Himself so wonderfully to this oppressed woman.

In the living room the farmer explained how it had all happened. On that Monday as usual he had taken his wife's breakfast up to her prison. However, for the first time in years he found her sitting on her bed in her right mind. She spoke to him clearly and distinctly and implored him to give her some other clothes to wear. He had risked doing this and had let her come downstairs into the house. The first thing she had done was to make herself look presentable, and then she had cleaned out the house. She had since cooked the meals and worked in the house for the whole week. The farmer had wondered all the time if she would have a relapse. But she had not and had remained in good health.

A week later the farmer was again at the gate waiting for the teacher. "Come in", he called. "There is something more to see." They went into the house and there at the piano was his wife. She had been an excellent pianist and could now play again. The farmer said that she had also done some shopping in the village and was still looking after the housework excellently. Three weeks after the wonderful deliverance the woman went to see her parents at Thüringen. There was much rejoicing. And so her recovery was complete and her previous troubles disappeared entirely. The teacher only once ventured to ask her about her illness. She said it was all very vague but she remembered two men visiting her. One of them had been black and the other white. The white man had called out, "Jesus has overcome", and she had afterwards been healed. About the teacher's visit she could remember nothing. He said no more, but inside he praised the Lord. The woman has continued in good health for a number of years now; and so

Christ has maintained His victory over the powers of the devil.

The next example was told to me personally by the teacher and reveals even more clearly the satanic powers of occult intrigues, although the victory of Christ is doubly apparent. This time I will let him tell the story himself.

168. A friend of mine was an insatiable reader. He spent every penny he had on books. The main subject he was interested in was occultism and he bought all the books he could on the subject. He was in the habit of reading and studying late into the night. The understanding he received in this way from the 'other side' and the wisdom of these 'prophets' held a tremendous appeal for him. He began to do certain recommended exercises and to eat the food they advised in the hope that he would become of 'purer blood' and attain a 'higher being'. Ultimately he hoped to receive revelations from the spirit world himself. For a while all went well. Suddenly, however, a rumour went round the town that he had gone mad. He had gone into a frenzy and had started smashing everything around him at home and threatening everybody who came near him. The man was placed in a padded cell of the psychiatric clinic. He raved and raged about like a wild animal. His cries were heard throughout the building. He was finally put into a straight jacket to stop him throwing himself at anyone and everyone who went into the cell. But in spite of all his raging his mind remained clear. He knew exactly what was going on, who was speaking to him, and what was said. But from within himself some terrible voices started to speak out. They ordered him to blaspheme the name of Christ and if he failed to obey he was terribly tormented. There was no doubt about it, he had fallen prey to the powers of darkness and was possessed of evil spirits.

The man's parents were Christians and they told their minister of their grief. A prayer group was formed to pray for the oppressed man. However, at first in spite of intensive prayer the man's condition only worsened. The voices only ordered him more vehemently to curse the name of Jesus. But the Lord heard the prayers of his children in the end, and after a few days he was able to leave his padded cell and go home.

Some time after this there was another disaster. He suddenly went blind. Again the prayer group prayed for him. Again their prayers were heard. His eyesight returned, but the demons had not finished with their victim. A little later they struck again. One morning the man woke up to find he was covered with a plague of leprosy and boils. The abscesses covered his body from head to foot. He was again admitted to hospital. His body emitted a terrible stench. No one could stay in his room. The Christians then prayed once more, and for the third time God answered. The stricken man was healed and allowed to go home. Yet the demons would not admit defeat. The next thing was that the man discovered signs of venereal disease on himself. For the fourth time he was admitted to the hospital. Now the doctors thought they had discovered the cause of the previous three illnesses. They prepared to operate the next day. But the man objected, saying that he had never done anything to get the disease. He prayed himself, and the prayer group also prayed. There was an improvement in his condition that night and so the operation was cancelled. The symptoms of venereal disease disappeared as quickly as they had come.

The next thing that happened was almost unbelievable. Both his hands and his feet became so badly twisted that he could not even walk. He had to drag himself along on crutches. The Christians recognised now that these extreme

forms of illness were demonic effects. They explained this
to the afflicted man and asked him if he had ever been
involved in occultism. Since he had led a reasonably moral
life up till that time he could not think of anything in
particular that he had to confess. It was then that this
group of Christian men noticed how many books he had
on occultism. His bookshelves which stretched all round
the room were full of them. The leader of the group was
alarmed at the sight of all the spiritistic and magic literature. The men told him catagorically that he had to cut
himself off completely from his occult literature. But the
man was not happy with the prospect, as he had invested
a lot of money in it. For a while he argued with them but
in the end they said to him, "Either you get rid of these
books, or else you remain the target for demonic attacks."
The man gave in. They burned the books there and then.
It took them some hours to burn all the books that he had,
and he stood there throughout the process lamenting his
loss. As they were getting to the end the man took hold
of one of the expensive leather-bound copies written by
Jacob Lorber and said, "Not this one. I must keep this
one." The others were adamant. They told him that he
would never be liberated unless he had got rid of every
one of his books. And so this volume too was thrown into
the flames. After this the man's condition improved stead-
ily each day. The terrible troubles of the past did not repeat themselves. A few weeks later on the advice of the
other Christians he went to a Christian convalescent home.
Under the ministry he received there he found Christ to be
his Saviour and experienced a complete renewal of his life.
The crippling in his hands and feet which had improved a
little since the burning of the books was now completely
healed. He later, after his deliverance in body and soul,
obtained the post of a technical designer in a large firm.

He married happily and continued, by the grace of God, to be a true disciple of Christ, being much used in the blessing of others.

The last four examples come to us from a well-known evangelist, known to me personally, who has kindly allowed me to publish them in this book.

169. It was in 1956 that a young married couple came to see me one day. They were Catholics, and they told me that the house they lived in was haunted at night. They had asked their priest to help, but he had never heard of anything like this before and was unable to do anything for them.

The husband, a strong man and a builder, told me the following story. At a certain hour of the night the bolted door of their home would open suddenly and they would hear footsteps coming across the children's room into the bedroom adjoining it. Someone would then walk up to his bed and throw himself on him. In spite of the fact that he tried with all his might to defend himself by kicking and hitting out he was unable to prevent his being assaulted. The man said that he could not go on much longer, what with a full day's work and these nightly attacks to cope with he was being exhausted. His wife confirmed how that she had to live through these experiences although she herself was left untouched, as the attacks only seemed to concern her husband. They went on to tell me that to escape from this plague they had moved to another district of the town. However, they had hardly settled into their new home when the plaguing started again. A woman's voice had called out over the husband's bed, "You see, I've found you!"

As I was to discover this was a case of past occupation with the sins of sorcery. The man's mother who was now dead had indulged in fortune-telling and other secret arts. After explaining these things to the couple I encouraged them to repent and to come to Christ. I also asked them to attend the meetings I was holding regularly. After prayer and after calling on the name of Jesus, laying claim to the precious blood, they were both delivered of the plague.

It should be mentioned that the man's nightly attacks were definitely not sexual hallucinations. The man was physically and mentally in perfect health. The problem was one similar to those often experienced on the mission fields. Occultly subjected people are often demonically tempted and troubled. An example which parallels the story we have just mentioned is the so-called 'fox-possession' in China. This is explained in the paragraph headed 'Incubi and Succubae' in the book *Christian Counselling and Occultism*. Counselling experience teaches one that psychiatric treatment is of no use in this area. Only Christ has the power and strength to overcome the dark powers of Satan. The cross of Golgotha stands as a beacon of victory over the dark attacks of the devil. This was revealed in the case of the Catholic family, for once they had stepped onto the ground of Christ's victory, they found deliverance.

170. In July 1945 a woman in great distress came to see me, and asked me for help. She told me of the strange way in which both of her daughters had been taken from her. When the elder girl had been six weeks old she had begun to have fits of crying, and this lasted till she was 18 weeks old. The doctors could find no reason for the crying and were unable to be of any help. The woman had then gone to see a mesmeriser and through the treatment received the child's condition improved somewhat. But now some strange things started to occur. One night as the child was next to her in the bed she stretched her hand out to put it on

the child's head. Suddenly she felt something like the fur of an animal. She put the light on at once but saw nothing. The child had been about three and a half at the time. The child was also quite religious and some days before it died it said to its mother, "Mother, read the Bible." On the 14th October 1941 at about ten o'clock in the morning a bird began to sing just outside the window. The child then died.

In 1942 the woman was again pregnant. At this time another woman came to the house and through card-laying she told the mother, "You are going to have a girl." After this the woman had a terrible dream. In the dream she was seized by some horrible woman who said to her, "You are going to have a little girl but I will kill her again." Well, soon after this she gave birth to the expected child. It was a girl. When she was six weeks old she nearly choked. The mother again sought the help of the mesmeriser. On the 18th October 1944 the same bird as before began to sing outside the window. The child suffocated in the mother's arms. It was 15 months old. A doctor who examined the child could find nothing wrong with it.

The woman now had one other child, a 14-year-old boy. However, through having her fortune told she learnt that he too was to be taken away from her. It was her fear of losing him that had brought her to see me in Strasbourg. She said to me, "As I was just outside your door I heard a voice quite clearly next to me say,' 'What are you doing here? You are a religious woman. You've been baptised and confirmed, and you go to church each week. What more can you do?' I didn't let this voice stop me though. Will you help me please, now that I am here?" After a brief conversation I encouraged the woman to repent and change her old way of life. She then confessed her sins and handed her life over to the Lord. After praying with her she said

that it was as if a great weight had fallen from her should-
ers. I was able to tell her in the name of Jesus that her
sins were forgiven, and I added, "Just believe, and your
son shall live. The devil is unable to take him away." She
returned home joyfully. We too can praise the name of the
Lord for His grace and His victory.

Since the time I have just mentioned the young lad has
grown up to be an excellent Christian and teacher. He
takes an active part in encouraging people to go to church
services and other similar meetings and through the many
coach parties he has thus arranged many people in his
neighbourhood have been blessed. His mother has since then
given birth to a fourth child, in 1946, and it has given them
much joy as it has grown up. The original oppressions and
troubles have disappeared since the time when the woman
placed her life under the control of Christ.

Concerning the example I have just related, there is a
great divergence of opinion amongst doctors and theologians. In general doctors consider a phenomenon of this
nature to be the outworking of some physical illness, and
would like to look upon it as a purely immanent event
(explicable entirely in terms of the natural world). A great
many theologians, especially those of Bultmann's school of
thought, would agree with this opinion. They look on stories in the New Testament which are similar in character
to this, as merely the products of that age, without realising
that the selfsame demonic oppressions are frequently to be
found in people today. For myself I cannot agree with
them. When one counsels severely oppressed people one is
confronted with an entirely different state of affairs. Some
oppressions just cannot be explained away on purely medical grounds, and neither can they be dismissed by a rationalistic theological explanation. The answer can only be

found through Christ. In the example of the woman I have just related there is a definite connection between the sins of sorcery and the consequent demonic effects. The woman had already as a child been healed by a magic charmer. At 18 she had been to a card-layer who had prophesied that she would suffer from a grave illness. And for four years following this visit she had actually had tuberculosis of the lungs. Counselling further revealed that the woman's mother had also been mixed up in sorcery, having been actively engaged in magic herself during her life. And in addition to all this the family lived in a village which was well-known for its practice of black magic. Some time after this counselling session with the woman I was able to hold a mission in this particular village. In spite of the opposition that was to be expected, the Lord sent a revival there. Many families were converted. As well as this the relatives of the family in question also came to the Saviour. At the same time many serious cases of sorcery were revealed. Christ nevertheless proved Himself again to be the victor over all the wiles of the evil one. In this village today there is now a real fellowship of genuine disciples of Christ.

171. In 1954 I visited a man living in Strasbourg. He told me that he was terribly plagued. In his distress he had gone to see the minister of his local church but the man had not been able to help him. Instead the minister had referred him to me. When he told me about himself my reply was, "Only the Lord Jesus Christ can help you."

The man had already been in a mental home and dreaded the thought of returning there. His brother too had been in an institution for a number of years. As I soon discovered, he was enmeshed in all kinds of sins of sorcery. As a child his parents had practised charming in their house, and he had later visited fortune-tellers and similar people

himself. Only recently when he had been ill he had been
visited by a disciple of the false Christ, Georges Roux of
Montfavet. This disciple had asked for three small pieces
of linen cloth, and then had dipped them in some holy water
and laid them on three spots of the patient's body. He had
then prayed for the man under the laying on of hands.
Since that time he had been badly plagued. At night when
he had gone to bed he had experienced a continuous crawling
feeling in his pillow and mattress, and it even continued
when he slept in another bed. During one of his visits to
me I asked him involuntarily if he wore anything about his
neck. "Yes", he replied, and he opened up his shirt to
reveal two amulets there. One of them had come from
another man who worked in conjunction with a medium.
In it was a piece of paper on which were some mysterious
signs together with crosses and a proverb. This piece of
paper was itself sewn into a small piece of cloth. The second
amulet contained a copper coin, a piece of wax about the
size of a finger nail, again both sewn into a piece of cloth.
He had obtained this second amulet from a cloister where
he had gone to seek help. They had given it to him after
a ceremony of consecration, and they had told him to
carry it close to his breast. In addition to this he had also
been given some consecrated wax which he was told to
dissolve and drink in his coffee.

I took the two amulets away from the man and burnt
them in front of him on the kitchen stove. He asked in all
seriousness and quite anxiously if any more misfortune
would come upon him as a result of this. After giving him
some basic teaching I earnestly encouraged him to repent
and to set his life in order, both in the eyes of God and
in the eyes of man. He said he was ready to give his life
to God. Then followed a confession of his sins which
brought to light some of the most dreadful sins and abom-

inations. Over a period of weeks and months he returned again and again to see me in order to confess new sins which had been brought to his mind, and he had to return a lot of stolen property. New demonic attacks occurred, but in the end he found his peace with God. Today as a Christian he is still active in the church to which he belongs.

As a result of sins of sorcery this man had had some terrible experiences in his life. Yet wherever the oppressions and the burdens of the devil have grown mountain high, the grace of God reaches even higher. Around the cross of Calvary there lies a field of force wherein those bound and fettered by sin find release and joy.

172. In 1956 I was asked to counsel a widow who had been left completely alone in the world. When she first visited me she told me the following story. Her husband had worked on the railways and had died in the previous year. Since then her only means of support had been through her 39-year-old daughter. This daughter had been a talented and gifted woman but had suddenly started to act very strangely. She was finally caught by the police in a cemetery in the process of exhuming her younger brother who had been dead for some years. She had had a human bone in her hand which she had only allowed them to take away when she got to the hospital. While this daughter was at the hospital the mother discovered that one of the rooms of the house was locked, and the key was missing. It was later found on the daughter in the mental hospital.

When the mother unlocked the room she discovered a number of books on sorcery there. She then realised that both her husband and her daughter must have used these books to practise sorcery. She had known nothing of this before and was herself opposed to the practice of such things. On checking up with the relatives I discovered that the daughter had already as a child been healed through magic charming on several occasions. The mother burnt the books immediately. But that same night she was terrified out of her sleep by some dreadful rumbling and heavy knocking noises. She simultaneously heard footsteps in her bedroom accompanied by knocks and scratching in the walls and furniture. In her distress she called on God and prayed some verses of a hymn. The noises did become somewhat quieter after this but they failed to go away altogether and they recurred each night.

After explaining the idea of repentance and faith to her, the woman expressed a willingness to trust in Christ. I encouraged her to really put her faith in Him, and to call upon the Lord in her distress. After this, matters improved somewhat, but later I received a letter saying that she could no longer get any peace. I felt constrained to go to the house in question. When I arrived I immediately commanded the spirits in the name of Jesus Christ to leave at once. The troubles ended and there were no more disturbances in the house thereafter. This was a literal fulfillment of the words, "With authority he commands even the unclean spirits and they obey him" (Mark. 1:27). We can praise the Lord that he still sets the prisoners free even today.

IV. What the New Testament says

We will now turn our attention following these examples of deliverance to a brief study of what the New Testament has to say about this matter. The following is therefore not a detailed treatment of the subject of deliverance. I have gone into the problem more fully, both in my more comprehensive work *Christian Counselling and Occultism* and at the end of the chapter on spiritism in the book *Between Christ and Satan*.

a. First of all one must be very careful in one's diagnosis before one sets out to treat a person whom one believes to be occultly subjected. A mentally ill person does not only need the encouragement that comes through counselling but also actually needs medical help. An occultly subjected person, however, should only be counselled by a Christian worker who is backed up by God's own authority. A clear line of demarcation can be drawn between mental illness and occult subjection. Psychiatrists and psychologists cannot be expected to understand this, as for them the only laws that are really valid are the purely physical laws. However, a psychiatrist who is not just a nominal Christian but is in fact a genuine disciple of Christ would be an exception. (Phil. 2:27, 1 Tim. 5:23, 2 Tim. 4:20.)

b. Only Christ can deliver a person from occult subjection. An oppressed person who is not prepared to follow Jesus Christ should not expect to find any form of relief. (Col. 2:15, Eph. 6:16-17.)

c. Although an open confession of sin is not obligatory it is urgently advised. Confession in fact means that the things that are hidden (occult means hidden or secret) are brought into the light of God. (James 5:16, Acts 19:18.)

d. Prayers of renunciation have been known and used in the Christian Church for the last 2000 years, and they also play a part in deliverance. They can sometimes take the form, "In the name of Jesus Christ I renounce Satan and his ways and pledge myself to Jesus Christ my Lord and Saviour for time and for eternity." Through a prayer of this nature the secret pact with the powers of darkness is officially and legally broken and abandoned. But remember, such a prayer should never be used superstitiously or as if it were a magic charm. It must come from the heart as an act of devotion to the Lord. (Matt. 6:7.)

e. To command in the name of Christ should never be done rashly or hastily. If it is, the suggestion of the idea of possession can build up in the mind of the oppressed person. And to command without spiritual authority is useless. (Acts 19:13-17, 16:18.)

f. Two special methods of help come to us through prayer and fasting (Matt. 17:21), and the small prayer group (Matt. 18:19). Some Christians without any outward show set apart days on which they are accustomed to pray and to fast for special needs. Small prayer groups are also of particular importance. The subjected person can himself be taken into the group which might consist of two or three people who have met together with the express purpose of praying for him. At best they should meet two or three times a week until the oppressed person is delivered.

g. Anyone who is finally delivered must remain on the alert afterwards. The powers which are driven out of a person have a tendency to return if one is not careful (Luke 11:24). It is necessary to put on the whole armour of God (Eph. 6:16f). If a person is later troubled again he must at once through faith place himself under the protection of the blood of Christ (1 Peter 1:2). To seek the help of a counsellor is always good, but it must be emphasised that the counsellor must himself be a person who has had at least a little experience in the occult field. Furthermore, the one who is delivered belongs within the Church, within the place where the Word of God is honoured and where prayer is wont to be made, and where the Lord is remembered in the breaking of bread (Acts 2:42). The blade of wheat waving in the breeze depends to a large extent on the other blades for its support. Standing alone it would soon snap off and perish. (Eph. 3:10.)

Yet one thing must again be underlined: the final victory belongs to the Lord. "The right hand of the Lord is exalted, the right hand of the Lord does valiantly."

Christ's Church is travelling across a bridge which spans the whole world. This bridge is rooted and grounded on the one side on Golgotha and Easter morning, and on the other side on the sure and certain return of Christ together with the final fulfillment of the purposes of God. Beneath the bridge a foul and odious stream ferments and stagnates. Yet as the evil vapours ascend, the Church continues her march through these poisonous clouds of satanic deceit and deception. The danger is ever present of having one's view obscured by the — now and then so attractive — poisonous breeze. Indeed many are befogged and, losing their zeal and their aim, they stumble headlong into the simmering morass below. Above this abyss are written the words, "But as for the polluted, the sorcerers and all liars, their lot shall be in the lake that burns with fire and brimstone" (Rev. 21:8). The Church, so often confused, asks, "What is truth?" and is constantly threatened by the swirling vapours from below. We find watchmen on the bridge marching with the innumerable host, calling and pointing to the One who alone can say, "I am the Way, the Truth and the Life." There are those who through vigilance and through the grace of God are arriving at the goal, and from the far side there rings out the great cry of the victory anthem, "They have conquered him by the blood of the Lamb and by the word of their testimony" (Rev. 12:11).

Now to him who is able to keep you from falling
and to present you without blemish before the
presence of his glory with rejoicing, to the
only God, our Saviour through Jesus Christ our
Lord, be glory, majesty, dominion, and authority, before
all time and now and for ever. Amen.

BOOKS BY KURT E. KOCH

BETWEEN CHRIST AND SATAN
An investigation into 178 case histories of occultism and a discussion of how Christ provides victory over the powers of darkness. 192 pages

CHRISTIAN COUNSELING AND OCCULTISM
An in-depth study of problems involved in counseling people entrapped in the occult from the points of view of medicine, psychology and theology. 340 pages

DAY X
The present world situation is reviewed in the light of the nearness of Christ's return. 128 pages

DEMONOLOGY, PAST AND PRESENT
A discussion of the work of demons and illustrations of people who are involved in demonic activity. 162 pages

THE DEVIL'S ALPHABET
A review of 47 forms of occult superstition, magic, fortune-telling and spiritism plus New Testament teaching for deliverance. 158 pages

OCCULT ABC
To be forwarned is to be forearmed. Bringing to the reader an awareness of more than 70 occult movements and Satan's devices, this book discusses such topics as, acupuncture, clairvoyance, drug abuse, homosexuality, parapsychology, queen of darkness, rock music, scientology, spiritism, yoga, etc. The book does not minimize problems nor exaggerate them and provides a light to illuminate some pitfalls for the unwary to avoid. 356 pages

OCCULT BONDAGE AND DELIVERANCE
An aid to counsellors of people who are under occult
bondage and subjection. Offers Christian counselling
and medical diagnosis. 198 pages

SPEAKING IN TONGUES?
An outline of the development and spread of the tongues
movement with numerous case histories. 64 pages

WORLD WITHOUT CHANCE?
A study of the work of the Spirit of God through the
Gospel in many parts of the world. 96 pages